Recorded Fragments

Recorded Fragments

Twelve reflections on the 20th century with Daniel Bensaïd

Daniel Bensaïd

IIRE and Resistance Books

Daniel Bensaïd was born in Toulouse in 1946. He became a leader of the 1968 student movement and subsequently of one of France's main far left organizations (Ligue Communiste Révolutionnaire) and of the Fourth International. He is the author of *Marx for our Times,* Verso: 2010, *Strategies of Resistance,* Resistance Books: 2014 and *An Impatient Life,* Verso: 2015. He died in Paris in 2010.

RECORDED FRAGMENTS

Twelve reflections on the 20th century
with Daniel Bensaïd

English edition published in 2020 by the International Institute for Research and Education and Resistance Books.

© English translation IIRE and Resistance Books.

Edited by Penelope Duggan.

Cover design by Adam di Chiara.

Recorded Fragments is issue no. 68 of the IIRE Notebooks for Study and Research.

First published as *Fragments Radiophoniques 12 entretiens pour interroger le 20e siècle* by Editions du Croquant, 20 route d'Héricy, 77870 Vulaines-sur-Seine, 2020. © Editions du Croquant.

Acknowledgments in the French edition

The publication of this book is the result of the collective work.

Robert March, Jacqueline Guillotin, Come Pierron, Guillaume Garel, Marion Druart, Hegoa Garay and Olivier Neveux transcribed and corrected the interviews.

Thierry le Bail (tlebail@mailo.com) did the cover design.

Thanks again to Louis Weber and the publisher of Le Croquant, to the whole team of Fréquence Paris Plurielle and of the show *Les oreilles loin du Front*, Laurent and Gwenn from the group *Sous la Ruine*, Camille Jouve, Alexandre Guérin and Christine Poupin, Pierre Barron and Patrick Le Moal.

Pierre Barron and Patrick Le Moal (coordinators)

The audio version in French of the interviews with Daniel Bensaïd is available here: http://www.loldf.org/bensaid/bensaid.html.

Acknowledgements for the English edition

Bernard Gibbons, Dave Kellaway, Fred Leplat and Marie Stewart translated the book which was edited by Penelope Duggan.

Notes on contributors

Olivier Besancenot was presidential candidate for the LCR in 2002 and 2007 and spokesperson of the NPA from its foundation in 2009, while remaining a postal worker. He is the author of several books, including two with Michael Löwy. His most recent is *Que faire de 1917 ? Une contre-histoire de la révolution russe.*

Isabelle Garo is a philosophy teacher and writer specializing in the works of Karl Marx. She is the author of several books, the most recent is *Avec Marx, philosophie et politique,* with Alexis Cukier.

Michael Löwy is an internationally-known Marxist intellectual. He is honorary director of research at the CNRS in France. The most recent of his works is *Romantic Anticapitalism and Nature. The Enchanted Garden* with Robert Sayre

Arya Meroni and Hegoa Garay are feminist activists in Toulouse.

Olivier Neveux is professor of theatre history and aesthetics at the Ecole Normale Supérieure in Lyon.

Ugo Palheta is a lecturer at the University of Lille and author of *La possibilité du fascisme. France : trajectoire du désastre.*

Christine Poupin is an ecosicalist acitivist and trade-unionist. She has been a spokesperson of the NPA since 2011.

Pierre Barron and Patrick Le Moal who coordinated the book were also active in the NPA (and Patrick Le Moal in the LCR) alongside Daniel Bensaïd.

CONTENTS

1. Preface: Against a discourse of fatalism — 1
2. Some memories of the recording sessions — 7
3. 25 October 1917: The storming of the Winter Palace — 13
4. 15 January 1919: The murder of Rosa Luxemburg and Karl Liebknecht — 21
5. 17 July 1936: The outbreak of the Spanish Revolution — 29
6. 8 May 1945: The end of the war in Europe — 36
7. 1 November 1954: The red All Saints' Day — 42
8. 1 January 1959: The entry into Havana — 48

CONTENTS

9 | 17 January 1961: The murder of Patrice Lumumba   56

10 | 3 May 1968: The closing of the Sorbonne   63

11 | 26 August 1970: In memory of the wife of the Unknown Soldier   70

12 | 11 September 1973: The fall of Allende   80

13 | 10 May 1981: The election of François Mitterrand   91

14 | 9 November 1989: The fall of the Berlin Wall   99

15 | For a strategic Marxism   109

16 | Saving politics?   117

17 | Ecocommunism or ecology versus capital   127

18 | Taking leaps seriously   136

19 | The new wave of feminism   144

20 | Daniel, end and continuity   154

NOTES   161

Preface: Against a discourse of fatalism

MICHAEL LÖWY

Daniel Bensaïd was one of the most creative, imaginative and sharpest minds in the contemporary history of Marxism, in France and beyond. He had the gift of combining fidelity to our Great Ancestors – Marx, Lenin, Trotsky – with an extraordinary open-mindedness and boundless curiosity, which made him read with profit the memoirs of Chateaubriand and the biography of Joan of Arc, the sociology of Max Weber and the political philosophy of Hannah Arendt. All his writings are driven by the irreducible force of indignation, an indignation which, he wrote in *Les irréductibles* (2001), is a beginning: '[It is] a way of getting up and going. One becomes indignant, one rebels, and then one sees.'

We got a lot closer during the 1980s. I probably contributed to his discovery of Walter Benjamin, and he made me read Charles Péguy. We shared an attraction for Auguste Blanqui, about whom we wrote an article together. Admittedly, we still had some 'disputes', for example about Rosa Luxemburg, whom I preferred to Lenin… But our 'elective affinity' was visible enough for our Brazilian comrades to publish two volumes (in 2000 and 2017) of our mixed writings.

It is true that these recorded fragments do not have the literary brilliance of his writings, where each word was cut and chiselled like a diamond. They have, in exchange, the direct, spontaneous, refreshing style of oral interventions. Their publication is therefore a significant and welcome contribution to the rich collection of his work. In his answers to the questions asked by his friends we find some certainties, but also many question marks: for example, was the social revolution on the agenda in May 1968? This capacity for doubt is to Daniel's credit!

These interviews concern the 'short twentieth century' (Eric Hobsbawm) from the Russian Revolution to the fall of the Berlin Wall, including the German Revolution, the Spanish Revolution, Fascism, Stalingrad, the Cold War, the tragedy of Greek communism, the Algerian Revolution, May 68, feminism, the Black movement, Lumumba and African independence, the Cuban Revolution and Guevarism, Allende's Chile and Miguel Enriquez's MIR, the Mitterrand years. No doubt ecology is missing, but it is true that the question was not put to him.

Of course, this excursion into twentieth-century history is the work of an activist, far removed from any pretension of 'scientific' or academic historiography. It is the expression of a thinker who does not compromise in his fidelity to the ideals of communism, and to the revolutionary legacy of the October Revolution. He defines himself as belonging to a generation for whom 1917 'was still something that stirred'. In fact, the spirit of the Red October runs like a thread of that colour through all these talks, and illuminates, like a distant but ever-present light, each of his words.

Certainly, he acknowledges that the Bolsheviks of the Leninist years (1917-23) made mistakes: Lenin refused to discuss laws or a civil code, while the terrifying violence of the Chekist terror was being exercised without legal limitations. After the end of the civil war and the victory of the Reds, many exceptional measures could be suspended; however, there was on the contrary a hardening of the authoritarianism of the regime, with the opening of political prison camps in 1923. The same is true for Leon Trotsky, head of the Red Army: his book *Terrorism and Communism* (1920) is 'a frightening text in many ways'.

However, Bensaïd opposes, with the last of his energies, the conformist discourse which assimilates Bolshevism and Stalinism, proclaiming, in a kind of parody of biblical genealogies, that 'Rousseau begat Marx, who begat Lenin, who begat Stalin'. In fact, Daniel rightly argues, a world separates the October revolutionaries from the Stalinist counter-revolution (which exterminated them all).

An uncompromising revolutionary, an inveterate opponent of reformism, Daniel is no less opposed to sectarianism, which he criticizes even among those he admires the most: for example, in the tone of Leon Trotsky's attacks on the Spanish POUM or Victor Serge. And he acknowledges that his own current has been unjust towards Salvador Allende: compared to today's reformists he was 'a giant of the class struggle'!

It goes without saying that in a set of improvised and spontaneous radio conversations of this type, certain approximations or gaps are inevitable. Several concern the exchange on Rosa Luxemburg, to which I, as a 'Luxemburgist', am particularly sensitive ...

According to my friend Daniel, Rosa Luxemburg and her Spartacist friends broke with social democracy too late, after the Russian October Revolution of 1917 and the German Revolution of November 1918. But that is not quite right – what does 'too late' mean? Before 1914, neither Lenin nor anyone else proposed to the German left to break with the SPD. In fact, before the Great

War, Lenin believed in the orthodox Marxism of Karl Kautsky, with whom Luxemburg had broken as early as 1909. In January 1916, Karl Liebknecht was expelled from the Social Democratic group in Parliament. The Spartacus League was formed, initially under the name of the International Group, in a clandestine meeting in the same month. It had its own leadership, publications, etc. In April 1917, the 'centrist' wing of the SPD broke up and formed the USPD, the Independent Social Democratic Party, to which the Spartacists adhered. In January 1919, the Spartacists founded the Communist Party of Germany (KPD), and in January 1920 the majority of the USPD joined the KPD. In short, the story is a little more complex, and in any case the Spartacists were out of the SPD-majority long before the October Revolution.

Bensaïd mentions Rosa Luxemburg's criticism (in 1918) of the Bolsheviks, but mentions, above all, her proposal to elect a new Constituent Assembly. However, Rosa's most important criticisms concern the absence of *democracy* and essential freedoms (freedom of expression, organization, etc.), including in the soviets, which could lead to their bureaucratization. Another curious shortcoming : our friend quotes the famous pamphlet *Junius* of 1915 (*The Crisis of German Social Democracy*) of Rosa Luxemburg, but only as a document breaking with the Second International – forgetting to mention the watchword, so decisive for revolutionary Marxism, of 'socialism or barbarism', that appeared there for the first time.

In spite of these shortcomings – there are undoubtedly others – the whole of this panorama of the century is no less extraordinarily coherent and crossed by a powerful visionary breath. The fighting and critical spirit of the speaker gives these fragments an undeniable moral and political power.

The name of Walter Benjamin is not mentioned in these interviews, but his spirit haunts the whole.

For example, Bensaïd ruthlessly denounces the wretched fatalistic conception of history, typical of a 'vision of victors'. For this story of a *fait accompli*, everything that happened was inevitable and necessary. This conformist discourse of fatality denounces the constitutive perversity of the revolutionary project, inevitably destined for totalitarianism: above all one must not try to change the world! Let us leave things as they are...

Now, observes Daniel, history is made of *bifurcations,* nothing – Stalinism, Nazism – was played out in advance, opportunities were missed. The future cannot be predicted, it depends on our own actions.

This wager on praxis is not blissful optimism. On the contrary: Daniel Bensaïd, like Walter Benjamin, is a *revolutionary pessimist*. Benjamin asserted in his essay on surrealism (1929) that the revolutionary must be able to 'organize pessimism'. Daniel does not speak of pessimism, but he explains that his revolutionary gamble is a *pari mélancolique* – title of one of his most beautiful books. Why melancholy? Because of the recurrence of defeat: were not most of the great revolutionaries of the past – Emiliano Zapata, Rosa Luxemburg, Leon Trotsky, Che Guevara, Miguel Enriquez – defeated, assassinated? Was not the fall of the Wall in 1989 the end of the cycle opened in 1917?

It was here that Daniel parted ways with his friend and mentor, Ernest Mandel who – when he saw in 1990 the joyful crowds in East Berlin shouting 'we are the people' – believed in a new revolution in Germany. Eternal optimist, the historic leader of the Fourth International proclaimed: this closes a parenthesis, we are returning to the great era of Rosa Luxemburg. But, Daniel comments soberly, there are no parentheses in history... The unification of Germany will simply be a victory for capitalism.

Turning a melancholic look back on the twentieth century, Daniel notes the defeat of the great hopes of emancipation at the beginning of this century. In 1900, the socialists believed in a century of peace, freedom, social justice... At the end of the century, we must acknowledge our historic defeat, a social, political and moral defeat (Stalinism).

However, and this is essential, this melancholy in no way leads to fatalistic resignation. More than ever, shortly before his death, Daniel Bensaïd believed in the future of the revolutionary gamble. Of course, we are entering a new era, but we are not starting from scratch: we are starting again from the middle. And we are preparing for the next forks in the road, which are bound to appear...

2

Some memories of the recording sessions

**PIERRE BARRON, MARION DRUART,
GUILLAUME GAREL, GWENN SANCHEZ**

In the beginning we are four friends.

Two of us host every week the political and social news programme *Les oreilles loin du front*, on Fréquence Paris Plurielle (FPP, 106.3 FM), one of the last community radio stations in Paris. The other two are members of the LCR and activists in the same cell (local branch) as Daniel Bensaïd. They debate with him on numerous occasions and listen to his speeches. But above all they remember those meetings in the twentieth arrondissement of Paris, which became rituals at the end of the year, during which Daniel told a somewhat embellished story of the JCR which became the LCR. It was a bit like Uncle Daniel telling nice stories, it was militant and intimate at the same time.

The idea came up to do a series of radio interviews with Daniel, which would not be directly related to political news or the publication of one of his books. We decided on a somewhat particular format: 12 dates introduced by one of us, Daniel would give his talk without us necessarily asking questions or prompting. The duration of each episode would be more or less 20 minutes.

Daniel immediately accepted our proposal, and left us free to choose the events and subjects we would submit to him to evoke a twentieth century seen from his window. The recording would be done in two stages, the first session in 2007, the second almost six months later in 2008.

If certain themes were unavoidable (October 1917, May 68, the fall of the Wall in 1989, ...), the subjects and issues that we chose corresponded to the questions posed by the activists that we were.

Thus, around the figure of Rosa Luxemburg we spoke of antimilitarism, surely because the first Gulf War deeply marked our youthful commitment, particularly through opposition to French intervention. It was also because the second Gulf War was barely over, if at all. Today, one would no doubt question other aspects of Luxemburg's thinking, for example its criticism of bourgeois democracy, in a period of declining public freedoms in the liberal democracies we are living in.

In the same way, we approached antifascism through the Spanish War. We were then at the time of Le Pen *père* and we think of the threat of the extreme right as the heir to collaboration and the OAS, in its methods and its policy. Today, at the time of Bolsonaro, Orban and other Marine Le Pens, we would certainly pose the question of the fascist threat differently, as Ugo Palheta does (see his text in this book).

The choice of questioning the Algerian war of independence echoes a series of programmes that we made with guests such as Maurice Rajsfus, Jean-Luc Einaudi, René Vautier and especially the arrival of young historians who renewed the historiography of colonial wars (Sylvie Thénault, Tramor Quéméneur, ...). And then the history of the struggles for the emancipation of the colonized peoples is also the political history of Daniel and his generation. These questions have since become increasingly important: thinking about colonization and post-colonialism means thinking about the society in which we live, from the management of working-class neighbourhoods to the repeated outbursts against populations designated as Muslim.

We can still evoke the episode devoted to the second wave of the feminist movement: during the first session, a first recording took place. But we had considered Daniel's words as disembodied, too often confined to listing the successive positions of the LCR on the subject. We had discussed it all together and agreed to take up this issue again during the second session.

Recording the interviews

We record at home. We push the furniture around a bit. Fold out the living room table to place the microphones and a mixer. At the first recording session, which had to be delayed due to health problems, Daniel's thin face shocks us. We are saddened to see him so weakened.

But once the microphones are plugged in, speech takes its rightful place. Despite the fatigue, there is a crazy energy in his words. One of his concerns each time is to think about the possible bifurcations of the story, not to read the events in the sole light of the story written by the victors. One gets the impression that when he talks about Germany in 1918, France in 1968 or Chile in 1973, history is still treading on his heels.

Daniel only has a sheet of paper with a few notes for almost two hours of recording. And then, above all, we are impressed by his ability to get back on track to conclude at the end of the agreed twenty minutes, despite the many detours in his reasoning.

We were rather proud of ourselves but also a little deferential, happy to attend a private lesson. The atmosphere was warm, Daniel had kept his talkativeness and his taste for broadcasting, and we laughed several times even if we remained very concentrated during the takes. Between the recording sequences, we joked, continued the debate and enjoyed the many anecdotes that Daniel regaled us with.

We also remember the madeleines left on the table that he had not touched and the glass of Chablis that he had accepted, probably out of politeness, but that he had not drunk.

After the recording, we reworked the sound a little, Gwenn and Laurent, who were then participating in an industrial music group that has remained obscure, *Sous la ruine*, composed original music that would serve as the opening and ending credits for these 12 episodes.

Once all this was done, we broadcast on Fréquence Paris Plurielle (106.3 FM) every Wednesday night for almost three months, on the show *Les oreilles loin du front*.

These episodes were then rebroadcast many times. And then the recordings stayed on our hard drives and in our drawers, where they gathered dust and age.

In 2018, Patrick Le Moal borrowed these audio materials from us. The idea of releasing them was born. Ten years after Daniel Bensaïd's death, it is the occasion to publish this work.

Listening to it again, we can see that the past decade has profoundly changed our world and the way we look at it.

The absence of ecological issues certainly corresponds to their absence in our own reflections and commitments. Christine Poupin repairs this lack in her contribution to this book. But with 12 dates, we could only be partial and biased. And this radio exercise says as much about Daniel's lifelong reflection on the history of the workers' movement as it does about the period during which the questions were formulated.

In 2007-2008, we were just before the economic crisis of 2008 and its endless consequences.

Before *Charlie Hebdo*, before the Bataclan and the mass killings in the heart of Paris, before #metoo. We were before Trump, Bolsonaro (but Putin was already on the scene). We were also before the collapse of the Socialist Party. We were before the Arab springs and the new wars in the Middle East, in Syria, in Libya, which threw millions of refugees fleeing the chaos onto the roads and into the seas.

In retrospect we realize that the issues that structure our political life today are largely absent or have been profoundly redefined in the course of the 2010s, from the finiteness of the planet and climate issues to China's place in international relations, from the articulation of gender, class and race to the authoritarian drift of liberal democracies, …

We were already living in a period when the workers' movement as defined since the end of the nineteenth century was disappearing: neo-liberal globalization, changes in work, atomization of workers, decline of the organized forms of the workers' movement, managerialization of societies, etc. were phenomena already at work that we certainly had not fully grasped. But as Isabelle Garo says in this book, 'the past only makes sense in the light that the present casts on it'.

Listened to today, the questions asked are dated. We were still thinking in the twentieth century. Yet in 2007, 2008, it was already thirty years since the Berlin Wall had fallen.

So when we listen to again, we tell ourselves that we would like to continue the dialogue. It is a bit old-fashioned to say that, but one wonders who, in this political current (Trotskyists, to put it simply), can today offer such a rich reflection? In these complex times in which a certain sectarianism tends to replace lively reflection, we miss Daniel Bensaïd's open-mindedness.

And if the star of the October Revolution is today very pale, we will try to remember that we must do radio in the freest possible way and discuss as often as possible with people more brilliant than ourselves. And still struggle.

3

25 October 1917: The storming of the Winter Palace

Finding a starting point for the long history of the labour movement is not easy. One could have chosen 1864 and the creation of the First International, one could have taken 1871 and the Paris Commune. We have made a more academic choice, the date of 25 October 1917 and the taking of the Winter Palace.

In the middle of the First World War, in Russia, under Lenin's orders, the Red Guards took control of Petrograd on 24 October 1917 and on the morning of 25 October 1917, the Winter Palace was taken. It was also the turning point of the Russian Revolution and if we evoke this date, it is because this revolution opens a cycle, a page in the history of a century marked by the exercise of power by certain regimes that claimed to be socialist and supportive of the workers' movement. So it opens up a lot of questions.

What happened in October 1917 in Russia and what meaning can we give to these events today, almost a century later?

Why are we so interested in the figure of Lenin and, behind that, in Leninism – a key influence in the workers' movement in the twentieth century?

First of all, about the chosen date.

Indeed, the Commune or 1864 could have been good dates, even 1848, why not? But I think the choice of October is relevant, due its impact and the international repercussions that it had. It was one of the events that conditioned and determined almost the entire 'short' twentieth century, or century of extremes according to the different formulas of historians. From this point of view, both historically and symbolically, it is indeed a founding or inaugural date.

There are several issues and problems that arise when we examine the October revolution.

Today its star has waned to almost nothing so it is hard to imagine the influence the news, the 'good news', of October had in Europe or even internationally, as a double act of liberation.

On the one hand it was the first socialist revolution of the century and even to some extent of history itself. The anecdote of Lenin dancing in the snow when the revolutionary state that came out of October had lasted longer than the Paris Commune is well known and often repeated.

On the other hand, it was the idea that social emancipation was possible and, at the same time, that social emancipation went hand in hand with peace.

Because one of the great reasons for the impact of the October Revolution beyond the borders of Russia was indeed this idea of peace, of 'never again'. It is surely one of the main reasons why, for example, the communists won a majority at the Tours congress in France. I had an old uncle who had been gassed during the 1914 war, who found himself in the majority at the Tours congress.[1] One of his main reasons for voting that way was peace, never again! The Russian Revolution seemed to carry that message, along with a message of social transformation and emancipation.

Two 'readings' of the Russian revolution overlap.

There is a historical, or historian's, reading that goes into the event, to understand its dynamics, its contradictions, its difficulties.

The revolution took place in a devastated country. Russia was not very developed before 1914, further declined at the end of the war and deteriorated in 1921 at the end of the civil war. These were the conditions of scarcity, of damage, in which bureaucracy was able to flourish. Nevertheless, in the heat of events, there was above all hope, as there was in Germany at the time. We find in Ernst Glaeser's novel *Peace* the same aspiration, where hope for social progress and the thirst for peace are combined.[2]

On the other hand, the heroic epic of October has been superimposed on the historical record. We did not experience the event, we did not experience October, we only see bits and pieces of films. The image of October that we have in our minds is not the report we would have today on the television news, it is the *October* of Eisenstein, already a symbolic sublimation of the event, with the epic quality of his cinematography.[3] In fact it is also partly how the event was perceived, how it marked the imagination of hundreds of thousands, millions of people and not only among industrial workers of Western Europe or the United States. Warren Beatty's film *Reds* shows how, among Minneapolis truck drivers, the event was able to speak to both individuals and whole generations.[4] I belong to a generation where it was still something that thrilled us, that did not have the dubious image of today.

You brought up the problem of Leninism.

Today there is a kind of reverse biblical genealogy: if it went wrong, if we had totalitarianism, it is because this bureaucratic despotism was a virus in Lenin, which was a viral mutation from Marx, which in turn was in the DNA of Rousseau. So, it is all down to poor old Rousseau – if it is not seen as part of the human condition itself. In opposition to this we need to identify historical continuities and discontinuities.

There are continuities.

It is clear that today we can identify the limits in the thinking and political framework of people like Lenin and more generally of people from the October generation, a generation of activists who came out of the culture and ways of thinking of their time. In predominantly rural societies, the relationship between culture and violence is not what it is today. There is an alternative idea of innocent and liberating violence. After Nazism, the Gulag, the Cambodian tragedy, the genocides of the twentieth century, we have a much more problematic relationship to all that.

We must try to understand the Bolsheviks' approach: the very words themselves have changed their meaning.

After Pinochet, Franco, Salazar, the Greek colonels, it is clear that the connotation taken by the word today prevails over the old Roman definition. This can be explained in scholarly books, but no one understands it in terms of everyday language.

On the other hand, there is a quite a libertarian Lenin, that we are less aware of, the Lenin of *The State and Revolution*.[5] If he sinned somewhere, it was rather by the illusion that the state would soon disappear. There is even a letter from Lenin in reply to the People's Commissioner for Justice. The latter wrote to him saying: we are in a state of exception, the law is suspended, we may have to write a civil code, and so on. Lenin responded: It is not worth it, since the state will wither away, there is no time, the law will wither away with it, so there is no need to complicate life.

In fact, there was an illusion that if the revolution were to spread on a European scale, and that was the major factor, all these hierarchical forms of domination and power would fade away, not on a historical scale, if not immediately, at least in the short or medium term.

So the problem has to be put in context.

What is problematic in books like *The Black Book of Communism*, or Furet's books, is to read history as a logical sequence of ideas.[6] The examination of material living contradictions, social forces in movement and real historical problems is completely drowned out in a kind of purely intellectual logic, or purely of ideas. That is the fundamental point!

On the one hand we can think that everything that happened in the twentieth century was already written into the October Revolution, because – and this was the Menshevik political line at the time – the revolution was premature, because the social conditions did not exist, because you cannot force the hand of history, etc. It is like re-editing a film of October from the end of the reel, it was all pre-ordained so it was pointless trying in the first place. And I think this is the conclusion that many former communists or even communist party leaders came to.

Or on the other hand you can try to figure out what happened. It was not inevitable. How can you define an event, a revolution, let alone a revolution like the one symbolized by October? It is what happened and what did not happen but could have. Otherwise events have no meaning, everything is pre-ordained. There are limits of course. Not everything can happen, it would be a religious miracle if that was the case. Events take place, it is possible there is one outcome but that one is not inevitable. We can look at the conditions that existed, analyse what happened and the unfolding reality depends on what happens afterwards.

Otherwise we consider that everything that happened in the twentieth century, the defeat of the German Revolution, the defeat of the Spanish Civil War, everything is pre-ordained. In that case we may as well fold our arms and tend to our gardens.

My position is that historical processes are never completely closed, the game is not over, and momentum can shift in the opposite direction. In the case of the Russian Revolution, this happened several times, in the German revolution of 1923, in the struggle in Russia itself between the oppositions and the rising bureaucracy at the end of the 1920s and in the struggle against the Nazi rise to power in Germany.[7] These were all forks in the road during the inter-war period that were not played out in advance.

After defeats become cumulative, that is something else. But the conclusion we have drawn is that there is no continuity: there was indeed a counter-revolution, you can call it what you like, bureaucratic or otherwise, during the 1920s and 1930s. It is certainly not a question of ideas, which is demonstrated by the millions and millions of deaths, in famines, in purges, in deportations and so on. There is an element of discontinuity here that I think fully merits the term counter-revolution.

The problem is that even Left Oppositionists like Trotsky, did not fully understand this because they were waiting for a counter-revolution that was symmetrical to the revolution, that is to say, a violent process that completely reversed what had been done.

Now I discovered belatedly what Joseph de Maistre, who observed the thermidorian counter-revolution after the French Revolution said – which shows it is a good idea to read the reactionaries.[8] He said : 'a counter-revolution is not a revolution in the opposite direction, it is the opposite of a revolution.' There is no symmetry in the way in which a revolution finally degenerates. Thermidor is not the symmetry of 14 July or the days of September 1792. It did not happen like that in Russia either.

For us what is important, is to identify and to understand this discontinuity.

We can certainly have debates on periodization, how it started, how it was prepared or facilitated by certain weaknesses in the Bolshevik political framework.

A generally correct theoretical framework does not mean you are always right. The text written by Trotsky in the midst of the civil war, *Terrorism and Communism,* is in many ways frightening today.[9] It is Trotsky's bad side, the idea that the dictatorship of the proletariat is a state with emergency powers. Well, this may be necessary in certain circumstances, but when should the state of emergency end? In 1921, when the Civil War was won, many emergency measures could have been suspended. On the contrary, there was a hardening of the regime's authoritarianism and a stronger move towards a single party regime. I think that at that time they did not think of the question of political pluralism as a political principle. They had the impression that if the bourgeoisie had been suppressed, the proletariat would naturally be good and recognize its interests.

It took time to understand that, even after a revolution, the previously oppressed or dominated are not homogeneous and that therefore contradictions must be able to be expressed through the independence of the trade unions, political pluralism, and so on.

The last point perhaps is to know to what extent October 1917 was a key date not only because of the impact of the event but because it was also the fundamental point of division of the workers' movement, the dividing point between the Second International and the Communist International.[10] The lessons of October served as the foundation of a whole tradition of the workers' movement, with its good and bad sides.

Some think that the short twentieth century, from the 1914 war and the 1917 revolution to the fall of the Berlin Wall, was a parenthesis. After that, history comes back to the norm, if there is a historical norm at all, which is another matter. Once the parenthesis is closed, the division on an international scale which is the consequence of the Russian Revolution, the Congress of Tours, the Congress of Livorno in Italy, the split of the Spanish Socialist Workers' Party...is it nonsense today and should we return to the pre-1914 unified workers' movement?[11] This question is on the agenda, this idea is discussed in all the communist parties of today, renovated or revamped or not.

I do not think it is a parenthesis. We are entering a new stage, but in this new stage, according to a formula that is dear to me, we always start again from the middle, we do not start from scratch.[12]

4

15 January 1919: The murder of Rosa Luxemburg and Karl Liebknecht

Karl Liebknecht and Rosa Luxemburg were both members of the German Social Democratic Party. In talking about them, and especially about her, we can discuss many essential subjects such as democracy or national liberation struggles, but we have chosen to focus on their anti-militarism. They fiercely opposed the 1914 war in the name of internationalism and against the majority of their party.

Their assassination on 15 January 1919 by the Freikorps of the Social Democratic government was followed by the slaughter of many German revolutionaries.[13] Their death thus perfectly illustrates the opposition between reform and revolution which they helped to highlight in their political activity. The date also marks, perhaps, the beginning of the end of hopes for the extension of the revolution in Europe.

This is also a very significant date .

The dividing line between reformist socialists and a revolutionary current was determined essentially by their respective relationship to the October Revolution, how they understood it.

Rosa Luxemburg, as is well known, criticized certain aspects of the October Revolution.

Her criticism today is particularly interesting, especially with regard to the dissolution of the Constituent Assembly.[14] There were two forms of political representation. On the one hand there was the legitimacy of the soviets which came notably from the October uprising. On the other hand, there was an elected assembly whose majority reflected more the realities of pre-October Russia. Political representation was lagging behind the real evolution of events.

Rosa Luxemburg did not question the dissolution of the elected constituent assembly at the end of 1917, but her position was not to abolish it completely. She argued that new elections should be organized. Although she had strongly criticized parliamentary democracy, she said that we must take other things into account, that the election of the constituent assembly was not a bourgeois luxury, that it is also one of the conditions of healthy politics along with the pluralism of the press, etc. Otherwise a revolution can become authoritarian. I believe that she expressed a very strong political sensitivity here, an awareness of bureaucratic logic, of the logic of the apparatus in political parties, even if she had not developed a theory of bureaucracy. That would come later.

This ties in with one aspect of the question, which is that awareness of this problem had been slow to emerge.

There was a policy debate at the beginning of the century, and I apologize for going back to that, but it makes sense. At that time, everyone was in the same social democratic party.

Bernstein developed the idea that some predictions, perhaps unfairly attributed to Marx, had not been borne out:[15]

– while the working class became more numerous and more concentrated, it was not more homogeneous, that is to say that unity was not a spontaneous product of the sociological growth of the industrial proletariat;

– the middle classes did not disappear, they were restructured, but there was no simple opposition, between bosses, a handful of bosses and a mass of workers; society remained more complex;

– and then the state apparatus itself was no longer the simple policeman or gangs of armed men, there were the ministries of transport and postal services, etc.

So Bernstein thought we could gain positions in the state apparatus. But, as a result, the very strong idea took hold at the time that social democracy, according to Kautsky's formula, did not even have to prepare for a revolution, the revolution was something natural, the result of a maturing of society right before our eyes.[16] The role of the party is purely pedagogical, it must help consciousness to mature. That is more or less the function given to the party: to organize this consciousness as it matures.

The first clash over this came from Rosa Luxemburg. Not just her, but she was one of the first to raise it, in the light of the general strikes in Russia and Belgium for universal suffrage.[17] She restored the inventiveness and creativity of a spontaneous mass movement that is neither decided nor framed by trade union and political apparatuses. The movement comes from below, a socialism from below that upsets bureaucratic routines.

A second element of analysis was added.

We had to wait until 1910-1912 for this question to be addressed, that of understanding what the state apparatus is. Here, it is as much Pannekoek[18], a Dutch socialist, as Rosa Luxemburg who says: but we have misread Marx, in fact, if we look closely at certain classical texts, which, moreover, had been kept under wraps such as the *Cri-*

tique of the Gotha Programme, Marx actually says that the apparatus of state must be destroyed, that it cannot be made to function as it was conceived.[19] It is functional in relation to class domination. You cannot just take it over as a technical tool. We need a qualitative transformation, a destruction of the existing state apparatus.

That is why I insist on the fact that this awareness existed over time and it took the litmus test of the attitude of social democracy on the war to finally say that it was not just a differences of opinion with the party apparatus. There was something rotten in the party which meant that, almost as one man or one woman, in 1914 they rallied to vote for the war budget.

The whole debate on the reasons for the failure of the Second International was examined by Rosa Luxemburg, in her Junius pamphlet.[20] She drew out the correct conclusions.

This has a certain importance in relation to their assassination in January 1919. Among the reformists there are sincere people, including honest people, of course, but there are also potential assassins. Personally, I was completely outraged to hear Ségolène Royal[21] claim to be a partisan of Rosa Luxemburg. I am not saying that she would pass us over to the firing squad, but she should at least have had the honesty to say that it was still the good old Social Democrats of the time who murdered her.

The problem, I believe, lies in the development of an alternative orientation and an understanding of the bureaucratization of the social democratic apparatus that had taken place over a period of fifteen years. As a result, unlike what happened in Russia, the revolutionary component that existed in the mass German social democratic party did not enter the war with an independent project.

It is usually said 'they did not vote the war credits', ... but only in the second vote. But even Liebknecht voted them in the first vote, yes, out of discipline, however we want to look at it, but he voted for them in the first vote.[22] And that is a big problem.

One can understand the inertia, German social democracy almost existed as an entire counter-society.

It had, I do not know, 150, 180 daily newspapers, newspapers in all the regions (the *Länder*), with a colossal trade union and parliamentary apparatus.[23] How can one break with such a force? One always hopes that it will be corrected or straightened out. But the revolutionaries had not realized that this break was inevitable... The German communist nuclei came out of the war weak at first. They were scattered and dispersed and to a certain extent with a leftist reading of the Russian Revolution, a somewhat putschist interpretation that was to last for some time in the German communist party. The kind of artificial insurrection of March 1921, ended in catastrophe and meant the Communist Party lost half of its membership in a few weeks.[24]

This also informed the Communist International's thinking on how to correct this juvenile or infantile impatience, however you want to define it, which existed at the time.

For example, one of the elements that served as a pretext for the offensive against the Spartacists, the embryo of the German Communist Party, in January 1919, was the occupation of the headquarters of the *Vorwärtz* newspaper, the organ of German social democracy.[25] This action, with which Rosa Luxemburg did not agree, precipitated the confrontation in unfavourable circumstances. It did not in any way justify the assassination, the deployment of the *Freikorps* but it was in a context of civil war.

Was the game effectively over with the decapitation of the nascent German Communist movement? It remained a significant political current. We now know how long it takes to develop a culture, a militant community. Having broken with the social-democratic majority very late in the ferment of the Russian Revolution and the end of the war, we have a party that was still barely under construction, that had just adopted a programme, etc. It is an open debate, but I believe that this assassination greatly jeopardized the building of a political leadership.

The term is not often used in France, but in Italy there is the idea of the leading group, there has always been a debate on how the core of the Italian Communist Party was formed.

This is something that has a certain importance in the history of a party.

There is a German revolutionary sequence that goes from 1918 to 1923. The ultimate conclusion of the German Revolution was the failure of the German October of 1923.

Perhaps the opportunity was lost before, but it was lost at several moments.

You rightly say that, symbolically, it was of course the assassination of Liebknecht and Rosa Luxemburg. But a few months or weeks later Jogiches was murdered.[26] So a whole part of the militant team was lost. They lost more leaders after the action of March 1921. Paul Lévy, we can say, after the fact, was an opportunist, but that was not Lenin's position.[27] On the March 1921 action he says: 'Many people lost their heads, but Paul Lévy, at least, had a head to lose. The others were scatterbrains.' The others... some of the Komintern cadres in particular.[28]

Then there is the famous story of the insurrection of October 1923, which is recounted as part of the Hamburg tragedy in Jan Valtin's book *Sans patrie ni frontiers* (published in English as *Out of the Night*).[29]

It is true that in politics, the consequences build up. This does not mean that the cycle was over, but it did make it much harder to get back on track. January 1919 probably affected March 1921 and October 1923.

But the consequences of all this are huge.

It is incalculable for the history of the twentieth century, not only for Germany and Russia. The whole strategic perspective of the Bolsheviks was that the Russian Revolution was the start of a European revolution. We had not started at the right end, but we had no choice. We were not deluding ourselves because if we look at what happened a few years later with the workers' councils of Turin in Italy, with the Republic of Bavarian councils in Germany, with the Republic of Hungarian councils and with the movements in Austria, there was more or less a European revolutionary or pre-revolutionary situation.[30]

The failure of the German Revolution conditioned the century and probably, almost certainly, determined the conditions for bureaucratization. It would have taken place in Russia, but perhaps not with the same results. Above all, this failure provided some of the conditions that led to Nazism.

The cost of revolutions and civil wars is often evaluated, even in facts and figures, but generally we forget to calculate the cost of lost revolutions, of revolutions not made.

Humanity paid an exorbitant price in the twentieth century for the failure of the German Revolution with the victory of Nazism and the Second World War.

That is why the symbols of Rosa Luxemburg and Karl Liebknecht are still so strong today... I was at the demonstration in Berlin in January 1968, which was an international demonstration for Vietnam. Berlin was cut in two, you had to cross a part of East Germany to get there. It was very moving. We were, in January 1968, half a century minus one year from the anniversary of the assassination of Rosa Luxemburg. In addition to solidarity with Vietnam, with the German student movement, etc., the symbol of this demonstration was also a tribute to Rosa Luxemburg.

5

17 July 1936: The outbreak of the Spanish Revolution

On 17 July 1936, the Spanish garrison in Melilla led by Franco revolted against the Popular Front Republican government elected in February 1936. This date marked the beginning of the Spanish Revolution, which would end in March 1939 with Franco's victory and the establishment of a dictatorship that would last 40 years.

In order to fully understand what happened in Spain at that time, it is important to take a brief look back. After the butchery of the First World War, the trauma was immense and long-lasting. The old bourgeois democracies (France, England) were weakened and were concerned about the development of organizations which supported the October Revolution. The German Revolution was crushed. In December 1920, the civil war in the fledgling Soviet Union ended. Lenin died in 1924, allowing Stalin to rapidly implement his theory of revolution in one country and eliminate all forms of opposition.

It was in this context that organizations identifying as fascist, along the lines of the regime established by Mussolini in Italy in 1922, developed during the 1920s. Dictatorships multiplied in Europe: Portugal, Romania, Poland, Hungary, but also in the rest of the world, including Brazil and China. In 1933 Hitler took power in Germany.

What do you think about the Spanish Revolution today?

What consequences did this defeat have on the world and on the workers' movement given the importance that anti-fascism has had and still has today in the workers' movement?

With regard to the Spanish Revolution itself, the big question that has been asked and is still being debated is how a civil war in defence of the Republic and democracy in response to Franco's military coup d'état could be combined, without taking more radical steps, with the deepening of the dynamics of the social revolution. This was the fundamental dividing line, whether or not you could defend the republic without further radicalization. The basic political position defended mainly by the Communist Party, which had the backing of the Soviet state apparatus, was that more radicalization was not needed.

The Communist Party was young and relatively weak. It drew heavily on its material support, especially military support, from the Soviet Union. It had a line which at the time of the Popular Fronts was all about the defence of democracy, with the idea that any dynamic which tended to deepen the social content of the Spanish revolution in the context of the civil war would be a factor of disorder, division, and weakness against the discipline necessary for a relatively conventional army to stand up to Franco's army.

That is what it was all about, what were the real opportunities for the Spanish progressive forces in this situation...

The problem cannot be reduced to that, because the internal balance of power, the international relations were such that the possible victory of the Spanish Republic, of the Spanish Revolution, was in any case uncertain for at least two reasons.

On the one hand, the policies of the European democracies. One of the great crimes of these democracies, including where there were socialist or social-democratic governments, was their non-intervention. At the same time Germany and Italy intervened openly (for example in Guernica[31]), including with forms of aid that were sometimes somewhat hidden. In the end, it can be said that the social democrats intervened everywhere except where it was necessary. Everywhere in colonial wars, always sending troops to keep control. Not in Spain, where to a significant extent the fate of Europe and probably of the Second World War was actually at stake. This explains the extraordinary echo of the Spanish Revolution in literature, from Hemingway to David Goodis, Malraux or Bernanos. It is an event that is also a defining moment of the century, with distant echoes such as in Malcolm Lowry's *Under the Volcano*, where the refrain is: 'We must send weapons to Republican Spain'.[32]

This is the major point and it is also a test of the different political orientations, regardless of the unquestionable heroism and sacrifice of the Communist Party's militants and fighters. But it was a political line that probably had a very heavy responsibility for the defeat. Now the whole history is better known. During a long period it was known essentially by libertarian circles, the left-wing opposition circles or the readers of Orwell and his book on free Catalonia.[33] We now have the film of Ken Loach which is inspired by Orwell's book.[34]

We have discussed the assassination of Rosa Luxemburg and the consequences for Germany, but the fate of the Spanish Revolution was partly played out in those days in May of 1937 in Barcelona. That is to say, in the repression of the libertarian and proletarian component within the revolutionary camp by the Stalinist leadership.[35] They restored military and state order.

Symbolically, and not just symbolically, we can say that May 1937 in Catalonia illustrates this. The whole history of the Spanish Revolution is also a test of different political lines.

Libertarian culture was very important for historical and social reasons. It was linked to the influence of Bakunin in the Spanish component of the First International and had roots in rural organizations in Andalusia, in particular. So there was a strong libertarian tradition which had its positive sides. That is to say, the experiences of self-organization and self-management, trying to solve the problem of the state by the simple abolition of power relations. In the final analysis the revolution is taken in the wrong direction: you do not want to get your hands dirty with power, you deny the problem of state power, but the problem catches up with you. You saw libertarians oscillate between an intransigence bordering on purism and then reaching 'realistic' compromises at a given moment. Sometimes there were even rather naive compromises with different components of the Republican clan.

I was familiar with the tail end of these debates because Toulouse was almost or partly a Spanish city. When I joined the Young Communists in 1962, there were more young Spanish communists than us. My first demonstration was against the assassination, the execution of Julián Grimau, a former leader of the Spanish Communist Party, in 1963.[36] At the Toulouse trades hall, there were the debates between communists, maybe a few Poumistas (I did not realize it at the time) and quite a few anarchists who kept re-enacting the battle of Guadalajara and the events of 1936.[37] It felt like repeatedly going over the same battles, but you could not avoid it.

On the side of the Spanish left opposition, there was a small Trotskyist left that acted essentially through the POUM and in debates that were complicated. The conclusion Trotsky drew from the victory of Nazism in Germany in 1933 was that the rise of Nazism, of fascism in Europe, would reduce the space in which social democracy could operate and grow. He thought the questioning of the parliamentary democratic game would undermine redistribution and negotiating compromises on which social democracy is based. The conclusion he drew, which was not necessarily wrong was, that, faced with this threat, social democracy, or part of it, would have to react, if only by a reflex of self-defence, by radicalizing to the left.

To some extent this did happen. There was the Austrian *Schutzbunden* insurrection in 1934 and other left currents did emerge in various places.[38]

With all his personal limitations Largo Caballero would appear today as a fanatical Bolshevik compared to current social democratic leaders.[39]

But the idea was that small groups had to be part of this radicalization of social democracy and, at the very least, accept that revolutionaries in the whole of Spain worked mainly in the Socialist Party – apart from the particular situation in Catalonia with the POUM. It was a difficult choice, no doubt about it. It is true that the POUM, if we compare it with revolutionary organizations today, must have had up to thirty thousand militants or so. In a revolutionary situation, this is not at all negligible. But with a very uneven development throughout Spain.

There too, Andreu Nin was not killed by Franco's troops.[40] Today, the kidnapping and assassination of Nin in Alcalá de Henares by the Stalinists is something that is proven, something that is not questioned in Spain. I am not saying that Andreu Nin would have played a role equivalent to that of Rosa Luxemburg. However, the organization underwent a double blow, since the other leading figure of the POUM, Joaquín Maurín, was arrested by the Francoists at the very beginning of the coup d'état. Others were executed in the Republican camp. I will not go into the hypotheses of Durruti's death, in any case suspicion remains and there was an undeniable settling of scores on the republican side to the detriment of its revolutionary component.[41]

I also believe that Spanish events sparked a certain sectarianism in Trotsky's writings at that time, which can be understood at least from a human, not to say psychological, point of view. One feels that there was despair that arose after every lost opportunity: the German Revolution of 1923, the Chinese Revolution, the victory of Nazism in Germany and now the Spanish Civil War.[42] Every lost opportunity brought the movement closer to catastrophe. This is one of the points on which Trotsky was lucid, he understood the logic of the coming war and even some aspects of it. For example, on the Jewish genocide, he was surely one of the few people in 1938 who foresaw that.

But at the same time, he was continuously struggling against the current and that, in my opinion, is a bad school, a bad culture. The tone of the polemics he led against the leaders of the POUM, who were revolutionaries who can make mistakes, or against Victor Serge is a culture of polemics with a sectarian logic.[43] This has to be said.

The reasons for this can be understood with hindsight. We are not in the eye of the storm, we have a certain distance that allows us to understand. But there is no doubt that this was a logic of despair. It was also aggravated by other events such as the Moscow trials and family dramas: the assassination (or not) of Sedov and the suicide of his daughter in Germany.[44] All these are human experiences that we can understand.

Finally, I believe that Spain should be compared to the Greek tragedy, even if it is not in the same historical period. For me, there were two experiences in Europe that are absolutely shattering. It is the way in which the Spanish Civil War did not just end in defeat, but by a defeat that was played out both in the Republican camp and in relation to the enemy. And then we see almost a worse replay of the tragedy, even if it is less well known, with the Greek Civil War, which was an absolute catastrophe involving a Stalinist party that even today has retained its DNA. It is the only one in Europe that has remained with that political approach. The Greek insurgency had state power within its grasp, but they were forbidden to take it and forced to lay down their arms. You have the photos of those who went to lay down their arms in village squares and stayed, were between 1947 and 1949, purely and simply murdered.

About the importance of antifascism, yes, there is an antifascist culture which is a legacy of all that, which was perpetuated by anti-Francoism. For us, maybe there was a microclimate in Toulouse, where the Spanish war was not over, when Frédéric Rossif's film *To Die in Madrid* was released, people came out in tears, it was still our war in the 1960s.[45]

Obviously, this is part of the culture of radical antifascism. I say radical antifascism to distinguish it from an ecumenical or minimalist antifascism that just says 'fascism is bad' 'it's wrong'…but does not really express its political line.

The Struggle Against Fascism is the title given to Trotsky's writings on Germany. It is a problem of political orientation, not just a problem of moral protest. There can be moral outrage, and that is a starting point. Basically, in the twentieth century, and *a fortiori* if the problem unfortunately continues into the twenty-first century, fascism will be defeated not just by defending democratic achievements, but also by progressive social policies that attack the roots it feeds on, whether in developed capitalist countries or in other parts of the world.

6

8 May 1945: The end of the war in Europe

At the end of the war, after the horrors inflicted by the fascist regimes, in particular the Nazi genocide of the Jews, a period of recomposition got underway. While western capitalist countries brought in a welfare state, and the Soviet bloc in Eastern Europe was established under Stalin's boot, there were considerable hopes among the working class. Progressive ideas and the influence of Communist parties may never have been as strong during the century. A very simple question: what was at stake at that point? Were there missed opportunities? What types of recomposition were taking shape?

It is a great debate.

Stalingrad is already a summary of the problems posed by the restoration of a certain capitalist order negotiated through the Yalta and Potsdam pacts.[46] I like to start out from literature. Vassili Grossman's book *Life and Fate* shows well how, in the battle of Stalingrad, a possible vitality of Soviet society was revealed.[47] Including hope, among people who were not necessarily oppositionists, but critical, that the initiative asked of them in the war against the German occupation would also lead to – their ideas might not have been clear

– a more open, more democratic society. There is a terrible sentence in this book: 'They had underestimated something; victors are not held accountable.'

The prognostic, or hope of Trotsky and Left Oppositionists before the war was a scenario similar to the First World War; namely that a bureaucratic regime like the Soviet one could not survive the ordeal of war and that the post-Second World War period would be a revolutionary situation as open, with a redistribution of the hand to play, as the aftermath of the First. In a certain way, Trotsky's position on the creation of a small International is also (in a different form) a remake of Zimmerwald, of Kienthal etc.[48] The small internationalist cohort had to be organized before the war's outbreak, to have a hope of coming out of it with something and to be able to face the opportunities that would not fail to arise.

Things did not go that way, because the Stalinist regime emerged legitimized by its military victory. I am borderline in generational terms, but the reverence towards the Soviet Union in 1950s France was impressive: when a Soviet runner such as Vladimir Kutz won three gold medals, or when Zátopek was brilliant on the track, or again when the first Sputnik took flight. It is hard to imagine nowadays, but people believed, they vanquished Nazism, so look what they can do. The Kolkhoz women with radiant faces in *The Cranes Are Flying* were not seen as ridiculous.[49] Relative to that, there was a (not very good) film *Rouge baiser/Red Kiss*, with nylon stockings and coca-cola, and American culture, which had to be boycotted.[50] It was a very Manichean world vision. But all that did come from the image conveyed, in part around the Stalingrad symbol, and afterward by the expansion of what was called the Soviet buffer zone, which could seem to be an extension of the socialist experience or pass for such at the time.

Some alarming elements were already there. The crisis with Yugoslavia began very early, in 1948-49, the Czechoslovak trials or those in Hungary of former brigade members who had been to Spain arrived very soon, less than eight years after the war.[51]

Contrary to the hope of a new revolutionary period, on the contrary it was a period of stabilization negotiated between two major partners, the United States and Britain on one side and the Stalinist leadership on the other, which established a discipline of disarmament within its own ranks.

In Spain, guerrilla fighters, including communist activists, held out until after the war, thinking that the dictatorships would not survive it and that the civil war would take revenge from 1945. They were called to order and fell into line.

Disarming the Greek resistance was perhaps the most dramatic consequence of this pact. This is why the Greek tragedy seems to me a good illustration of Stalinist policy. I know of only one book about that, although there are surely others, *Les Kapétanios* by Dominique Eudes, it is also in the novels by Tsirkas, *Drifting Cities*.[52] While there was much literature about the Spanish civil war, the Greek story remains little-known.

The Chinese revolution escaped this policy. For example, there was the opposition between the Varkiza agreement, which disarmed the Greek resistance and the Chongqing agreements in China which were supposed to be the equivalent.[53] Because Mao Zedong said the people's arms were the people's arms and not to be surrendered, and wavered between the Soviet Union's diplomatic interests and their logic. The Chinese communists had already gone through the experience of a compromise in 1927 and paid a heavy price.[54] It was a survival idea: we will not once again agree to offer ourselves up for an outright massacre. From that, there was a logic of their own, partly military, which did not necessarily have a fabulous social project, but which resulted in the Chinese revolution not falling into the trap. Moreover, it was China. There is also an element of scale.

The problem is that on the revolutionary side, if we remain in the European region and a bit more broadly, they lived through the Second World War – I believe that perhaps it was post-facto projection – awaiting a scenario as turbulent as the one in the 1918-1923 years after the First World War. And that is not at all what happened. The POUM disappeared; the British ILP, which was not a small organization, quasi-revolutionary left Labourists with people such as Orwell and others at the time, disappeared.[55]

And then, the Trotskyist current survived, but splintered. It split firstly over the interpretation of the situation. Some thought that the restart of a capitalist economy was only an interlude, in fact the war had not ended, in the short term we were heading towards another war and eventually a new world war, directly opposing the Soviet Union and the United States. Others thought that it was a lasting recovery; thus we had to prepare for a desert crossing.

But all the splits between different currents, or the appearance of a group such as Socialism or Barbarism – which was insignificant at the time, nowadays, looking back, it is thought that people such as Castoriadis or Lyotard contributed something, and it is true – are the expression of questioning that finally spread throughout the world.[56] How to understand the reasons and possibility of the survival of the bureaucratic regime in the USSR? Finally, this is what differentiated David Rousset, Castoriadis from other currents of the Fourth International who maintained the line that it was a degenerated workers' state.[57] But why did the degeneration last so long? How could it even spread so regimes such as those in Eastern Europe? And there were also defeats because in a certain way, this consolidation of the Stalinist camp – in both senses of the terms, what's more – had repercussions as far away as in Asia, in Indonesia and in the Philippines, or in Vietnam.⁵⁸ In 1945, there was the liquidation of the Vietnamese left opposition that was not a tiny group, in a Vietnamese Communist Party which did not toe the line either and continued its national resistance.

There was a real legitimacy of the history of the communist movement in the Third International that was borne by figures we know little about. Pandelis Pouliopoulos, founder of the Greek Communist Party, who became a left internationalist, was killed by an Italian firing squad.⁵⁹ One of the founders of Indonesian communism, Tan Malaka, who had organized Indonesian guerrillas, was also liquidated at the time.⁶⁰ A whole generation that could discuss the legitimacy of the Russian Revolution's heritage was crushed. This was also true in Eastern Europe; in Czechoslovakia there was both a surrealist movement on the cultural level and a left opposition. All of this was finally flattened by the steamroller. Meaning that the hypotheses on which the left oppositions were formed in the 1930s were disproved. Was this a fatality? An error in prognosis?

In my view, politics does not operate on prognostics, it is not laying bets ... what linguists would call performative: we say what would be desirable or necessary and attempt to strive to make it real and possible. Afterwards, as history is not written in advance, we observe what actually happens.

Finally, the economic recovery made it possible to bring in welfare states or social states, forms of Keynesian regulation that laid the basis for the social compromise, mainly in Europe, but also in other forms in other regions of the world.

It is not the same thing, but the Latin American populist states, Brazil's growth in the 1950s-1960s involved distributive mechanisms that were in part comparable, or the ECLAC theories on development for Latin America.⁶¹ This made economic growth possible via recovery. But it was also the bourgeoisie's great fear. It was not simply a present or because Keynes had a brilliant idea. They feared losing everything, in the 1930s, in the war or its aftermath.

Compromise is a way of ceding something so as not to lose everything. On that basis, it was a compromise that to some extent made it possible to limit social conflict for three decades, until the end of the 1960s, beginning of the 1970s.

One the one hand, this provided the illusion that capitalism had the means of mastering its contradictions and managing them rationally, and on the other hand, theories such as David Rousset's, that by different means, western capitalism and modernization, even under bureaucratic forms in the Soviet Union, would conclude with more or less the same society in convergent forms.

This is the conclusion of his major book, which nobody has read, *La Société éclatée*, yet this is one of the best books on the Soviet Union, concluding with this hypothesis of a convergence between the two superpowers.[62] We must add that he was not alone at the time. This was the era of peaceful coexistence when Maurois and Aragon wrote parallel histories of the United States and the Soviet Union.[63] The Communist Party sold them to us as a subscription promotion, in boxed sets. Every good Communist activist, even if they had only four books, had that one.

7

1 November 1954: The red All Saints' Day

On 1 November 1954, in Algeria, around thirty armed attacks took place in various parts of the country. It is known as the red or bloody All Saints' Day. This insurrection appeared as a decisive stage in the launching of the Algerian war of independence, firstly in its breadth but also because it marked the appearance on the political and military scene of its main actor, the FLN.

The war in Algeria and, more broadly, wars of national independence shook the workers' movement in France and around the world. New cleavages appeared, in particular around the attitude to adopt towards these movements.

Could you tell us what vision you had of the war in Algeria and, more broadly, try to deal with the historic relations of the left and colonial questions.

Well, this is directly our history.

It could be said that for my generation – I do not like these stories of generations too much, it is a little viscous but finally, well, this is a chronological account – we are, nevertheless, in part the direct or indirect product of this Algerian war.

Two kinds of problem crystallized around the Algerian war of liberation.

The first is the attitude of the workers' movement in the colonial metropolises in relation to the wars of liberation of anti-colonial movements. It is a fairly tumultuous history in which we find great divergences. There was a genuinely internationalist anti-colonialism, a veritable *élan* from this viewpoint in the early years of the Communist International, with the Baku congress.[64] The attitude of the young French Communist Party (up until the Rif war), was an anti-militarist one of sabotage of the colonial operation and this included work inside the colonial army.[65]

And then this tradition was, there also, gradually sacrificed to diplomatic gains and state interests on the international scene in the name, notably, of political alliances and, in particular, of the political alliances made in 1945, in the name of national reconstruction, of governments of national unity and so on. Which was reflected by a partly chauvinist national evolution of the French Communist Party. I say 'partly' because the affair is a little more contradictory. But in essence, it is quite evident. Whether on the Vietnamese or the Algerian questions, we cannot say that there was an active support for the Algerian liberation struggle starting from 1954.

Sometimes with theoretical alibis: is Algeria a nation? It is a nation in formation. Can we speak of national rights, with a whole discourse on the right to divorce or on the obligation of divorce: you have the right to divorce but you are not obliged to divorce. In any case, it did not amount to making the right to independence a question of principle. This was one of the points, moreover, on which at the time, not in a completely conscious manner, people became unhappy with and for some comrades became opposed to the line of the Party. It should be said that the Communist Party in France had the support of 25 per cent of the electorate, nothing comparable with today, and for somebody who radicalized, it was an engagement which was, I do not say inevitable, but broadly natural.

I was on the last demonstrations concerning the Algerian war and the central slogan was 'Peace in Algeria'. So, this was not explicitly a slogan of active support to the FLN and to the Algerians.[66] That support came very much more from intellectual circles with the appeal of the 121 which was not simply a petition appeal of intellectuals but a sort of moral engagement to active support, that is the sheltering of clandestine Algerians, a certain aid to the FLN.[67]

Then, finally, the launching of the Algerian war of liberation coming in 1954 at the time of the sealing of the defeat of French imperialism in Indochina, was a putting to the test of positions faced with a general movement of national liberation struggles in the Maghreb, in Indochina, but also, to a lesser extent at that time, in the Portuguese and French colonies in Africa.

This was the first problem, whose consequence was division in relation to the type of engagement, that is of solidarity with the whole of the anti-colonialist and anti-imperialist movement and of an active solidarity, not a tolerant solidarity in the name of peace.

We should be nuanced, all the same. The line of the Communist Party sometimes had complicated expressions, with for example, conscientious objection, the refusal to go to Algeria. Some Communist activists were imprisoned, like Alban Liechti. When I joined the *Jeunesse communiste* we campaigned for the liberation of Alban Liechti who had refused to bear arms against the FLN. There were very few cases of desertion, of people going over to the FLN.

The other problem was what could be expected from the Algerian Revolution itself. Was it a war of liberation for national independence 'full stop' or did its dynamic go much further in the direction of a socialist experience? The context there is important. The debate, I will not take it up here, was: who to support? The FLN which was in a certain sense more radical (it had taken the initiative for the insurrection) or the MNA of Messali Hadj which was historically more linked to a labour movement culture and which at the beginning, in 1954, was not a legalist organization.[68] There were divergences on what type of armed struggle, but not on the principle: the MNA itself was also prepared to wage military struggle.

Afterwards, I think that these are discussions that could be had more calmly because the MNA was transformed, in part, into an instrument of French colonialism. But this was not the case at the very beginning of the war, from 1958 onward it became thus. In their rivalry with the FLN, they in various degrees entered into a pact with the colonial authority.

The other problem was: what programme for the FLN? Was it a nationalist, indeed religion-based, programme? It was not completely settled, at the beginning, what the official reference point of the future independent Algeria would be, for example, a constitution referring to Islam as official religion. It became thus in the course of the war, partly moreover because of the way in which the OAS ensured, through the series of terrorist attacks on the eve of independence, that it became in practice difficult to imagine staying for the million people known as *pieds noirs*, who were not all colonists.[69] There were a number of people, I am in a good position to know it, who were of Spanish or poor Jewish origin. But the line of the OAS created an irreversible situation and finally favoured the definition of the state with a strongly religious reference.

And then the social programme of the FLN was not set in advance. There was the congress of Soummam which adopted a relatively radical programme in the area of agrarian reform, among others, around notably the figure of Abane Ramdam who was liquidated in the FLN's internal crisis by those who were known as the 3 Bs.[70] This was a bureaucratic settling of accounts within the FLN apparatus, but it had a political meaning. It liquidated the most social wing of the FLN which had a logic – we will not use big words – of 'permanent revolution'. The impact of the Algerian Revolution, with independence formally achieved in 1962, exactly echoed, for us, the dynamic of the Cuban Revolution, the Algerian scenario taking the same road. Was this possible?

It should all the same be remembered, in relation to Algeria, I do not know if we realize it, we speak today of something – perhaps the figure is rounded up in an exaggerated way – like a million deaths out of ten million inhabitants. It is huge, it is not a small thing. A society which has lived through this is already strongly traumatized. Also, the French had won the military war, they lost politically, but they inflicted such losses! The Algerian state apparatus thus did not emerge from an experience of self-organization of internal resistance but came notably from exile, from people who had been in prison like Ben Bella, but also like Boumédiène from the military apparatus built at the border, what was called the 'army of the borders'.

It is a little like a more modest version of what happened for Palestine: an external apparatus, financed from the outside and which came to finally cap a revolutionary process which had suffered quite a few setbacks on the ground.

So we had then a bureaucratic state apparatus. Initially, this did not stop Ben Bella from taking radical measures, the famous 'discourse on self-management' which existed, but based on a pinhead, with the ambiguity of the coup in 1965.[71] I remember, I experienced this, I was on an internship with the French students' union at the time, we spent the night glued to the transistor radio. We did not have a good understanding of what Ben Bella represented. We were in the *Jeunesse Communiste*. This had the air of going in the right direction, these were not communists as such, we did not really know where they were going, but all the same we intuitively felt the overthrow of Ben Bella was a real blow. But at the same time, this did not clearly appear as a reversal of the process inasmuch as a good part of the nationalizations of fuels and other sectors were continued or done outright under Boumédiène. So it did not appear as a brutal halt but as a continuity.

It should be said, perhaps it is forgotten, that the Algerian war of independence was for the movements of the 1960s or 1970s, a reference which was almost as strong as the Cuban or Vietnamese experiences. When I was in Argentina in 1973 I spent whole nights talking with comrades who said: 'we want to do the same thing as Algeria', with the idea that in Algeria they had won militarily. But no, it was more complicated than that. Algeria was a reference, forming part of this set of experiences of the colonial revolution. It should not be forgotten all the same that one of the founding texts for us was a speech by Che, the 'Algiers speech', during his visit to Algeria in 1965 where he took the most explicit position possible at the time in relation to the state of play and relationship of forces internationally and the USSR's policy precisely in relation to wars of national liberation in the colonial countries.[72]

8

1 January 1959: The entry into Havana

1 January 1959 saw the entry into Havana of the guerrilla army led by Fidel Castro and the fall of Fulgencio Batista's dictatorship. It marked, in fact, the symbolic and real beginning of struggles and resistance to imperialism in Latin America. From the 1960s onwards, these struggles mixed anti-imperialism, peasant self-organization and a renewed Marxism (which had an ambiguous relationship with religion) in a movement of emancipation. How can we evaluate the importance of the Cuban Revolution, of Guevarism and its influence on anti-imperialist movements both on the Latin American continent and on other continents?

The first thing that needs to be said in order to measure the significance of the Cuban Revolution is that, unlike what happened in Algeria, there were barely three years between the highly symbolic date of the rebel army's entry into Havana on 1 January 1959 and the proclamation of a socialist Cuba.

Therefore, for us, it was the first socialist revolution, with this type of political project, which had not been carried out by a communist party. To a certain extent it was done against the existing

Communist Party in Cuba, partly against it, since the latter had joined only during the last phase.

It was a shock that is harder to understand today, but which posed a major problem for all Communist Party militants. What is this rare bird, what is this movement of 26 July?[73] It was surrounded by a certain mystery. I recall, I remember reading old newspapers from the 1950s. It was all a bit exotic, there were guys with beards who claimed they were going to take power. In 1958, there were reports from American journalists about this handful of guerrillas whose story seemed to look like some Christian myth. They landed with eighty fighters, there were twelve survivors like the apostles, it is a great story. The very scenario of the Cuban Revolution, the rebel army, the dishevelled Che in Santa Clara, epitomized a romantic and epic revolutionary story.

There was a problem with understanding that but at the same time, we were able to say: 'but finally, there is a revolution that is not made by a communist party.' The first big problem for us, for example, without going into the personal reactions at the time, was that we did not know what it was all about. There was something exceptional about the figure of Che. First in 1959, we did not know much about him, then, in 1962-63, he began to be a symbol. One experience that struck me was hearing about the Cuban Revolution from Armand Gatti when he came to stage his plays in Toulouse. He had just shot *El Otro Cristobal* in Cuba.[74] Some copies of the film still exist, but we rarely see it and it is a shame because it is a lyrical film that expresses the spirit of the time. Gatti certainly was not a member of the PCF, he was a sort of melting pot of libertarian, communist, Maoist cultures..., a bit of everything, so it was like a real breath of fresh air.

It soon became clear that not only was this not a revolution led by an orthodox communist party, but that it had a delicate relationship with the 'motherland of socialism', the Soviet Union. There were complimentary speeches. Che had made a trip to the East. He had returned fascinated, among other things, by the way planning worked. I think there was some sincerity, but at the same time, as early as 1962, with the Cuban missile crisis, we felt, and this only developed more later, that Che's speeches were an indictment of Stalinism.[75] To a large extent, he could do this because he had more freedom of speech and fewer diplomatic obligations than Castro. The Algiers speech or the messages to the Tricontinental Conference in 1965 and 1967 are an indictment of the Soviet Union's international policy both on the forms of cooperation with the ex-colonial countries (in the Algiers speech) and on the type of solidarity given to the Vietnamese and Indochinese revolutions in 1967.[76] All this opened up a space of independence from Soviet 'orthodox' communism and the network of communist parties that supported it, but also from the Maoist discourse that had a considerable influence at the time with the illusions in the Cultural Revolution from 1966.[77] It gave us a material basis for saying 'there is something else possible'. Che's text 'Socialism and Man in Cuba' that a comrade had brought back from Cuba and translated in 1964, presented a different outlook, it was something new and open.[78]

What did this have to do with Marxism? Che had always had a rather enigmatic relationship to Marx. It seems that Castro had read Marx early on. But Che's texts and witness accounts of the coup d'état in Colombia – which is the starting point for what we know of today's Colombia, since 1952 – indicates that his formation may seem strange but also sheds some light on certain things. The French revolution and Jacobinism inspired him. He was an admirer of Robespierre and Saint-Just. That does not mean he did not know Marx. We do not know to what extent or how far it was ignorance of a different culture – a mixture of José Marti's Bolivarism, therefore of Latin American nationalist tradition, and of the French Revolution.[79] We know that the French Revolution, one only has to read Alejo Carpentier's novel about the Age of Enlightenment, is still a reference point in Latin America today, more so than here in a way.[80] Castro has a certain amount of Marxism that he did not go on about too much, possibly for reasons of diplomacy. As some of his comrades used to say, on some issues he is very laconic. He is very expansive in speeches and very discreet on other things.

On the religious component, I think there is a certain anachronism in your question. I am not saying that it did not exist at the time. There is a deep religiosity in Cuba, voodoo syncretism permeates the popular culture. But we were at a time when among revolutionaries, including anti-colonial ones, the dominant tendency was still one of secularization. This was true in Arab national movements, it was true in Africa among people like Amílcar Cabral and it was the case in Cuba.[81] So, on religion, they have always taken a low key stance. If religious practices remained, at the time there was no talk of something equivalent to liberation theology, i.e. a real social and political current of commitment that refers directly to a religious aspiration.

Then there is the after-effect of the Cuban Revolution, and there it inevitably meets currents such as that of Camilo Torres, one of the founders of the Colombian guerrillas who was a priest.[82] This is not the only case, there have been many others, such as, a little later, Ernesto Cardenal in the case of Nicaragua.[83] So there is that component.

Now the Cuban Revolution also had a very important impact on an international level. Today, in Latin America, for example, people are critical of Cuba on certain democratic issues, and rightly so. After the 1989 trials and the execution, following a Stalinist trial of Ochoa, a former Cuban proconsul in Angola, I read the minutes, they published them, there was no doubt.[84] We took a petition to the Cuban embassy with Gilles Perrault. But at the same time, the press here often presents Cuba as a kind of tropical Romania, which is wide of the mark. I believe that there is a necessary democratic battle in Cuba, but at the same time Cuba's legitimacy in Latin America is still there today. I doubt that Ceauşescu has ever inspired anyone on the revolutionary European left.[85] You cannot say that of Cuba, even today.

Even after the fall of the USSR, despite the blockade, they continued to stand up to imperialism. At the same time the Latin American left does not slavishly follow Havana, it has a critical view of Cuba. There is a prestige but at the same time people take a critical distance and understand that a society like Brazil is much more complex than Cuba and that what the Cubans say does not solve the trade union question in Brazil. But it is still part of the movement and part of history. Even more so today, if what remains of the embers of the Cuban Revolution is revived by what is happening in Venezuela or Bolivia. The process is not over.

Castroists themselves built up a mythology about the Cuban Revolution, relayed by people like Régis Debray in his 1967 book *Revolution in the Revolution*, which is a very particular reading of the Cuban Revolution. It systematizes a theory of the revolution that starts from a guerrilla base (*foco*) and then one has the impression that the base creates a rebel army which then conquers the country. There is some truth in this, but it is also a legend of the Cuban Revolution leadership, which, in my opinion, had an interest in building up the legitimacy of the 26 July Movement by relativizing everything else, including the tradition of the urban movement in Cuba, the Communist Party, etc. They wanted to assert that the monopoly of legitimacy was the 26 July movement, even though afterwards there was a unified Communist Party.

The lessons that were straightaway learned from this did considerable damage in Latin America: for example the idea that it is enough to have willpower. There is a culture of exemplary actions, both in the military field and in the economic field, as can be seen in the photos of Che bare-chested and carrying bags during voluntary labour. The economy is in a slump, but if we roll up our sleeves, it can work. In 1967-68, this led to the *Zafra* disaster targeting a harvest of ten million tons of sugar cane.[86] The Cuban leadership said since we are economically strangled, we are going to beat all the records for sugar cane production, specializing in monopoly production, but this is a sign of economic and agricultural dependence.

But the idea was that with willpower we can solve everything. You have a similar experience in China with the famous text on 'Yukon moved the mountains' which is an old Chinese legend recycled by Maoist rhetoric. But there was this idea and in Latin America it is the same: the conditions exist, what is missing is the will to act. We ended up with a massacre. We can draw up the list of martyrs in the 1960s and early 1970s: Yon Sosa in Guatemala, Camilo Torres, De la Puente and Lobatón in Peru, the Peredo brothers and Che himself in Bolivia, it was a slaughter of a generation, and it continued a little later in Argentina, Uruguay, with the Tupamaros and others.[87] They deserve respect nevertheless. They were people who wanted to do the right thing in their terms. We can discuss the rights and wrongs of it all once this is accepted.

At the same time, we must also take a balanced view of this period. If we took a superficial view we could get the impression that Che's escapade in Bolivia was a suicidal and completely irrational escapade, which it probably was not. One can say that there was very little chance of success. When you see the films on TV today that go to the scene, you think: 'But what was he going to do in this sparsely populated desert?' In fact the project envisaged an intercontinental guerrilla war and it was not that crazy. It was to create a hub between the region of Tucumán in the north of Argentina, Peru and Bolivia in a context of the 1960s where, it was difficult to see at the time, that perhaps the wave of national liberation struggles was running out of steam. But that was difficult to get a grasp of on the ground. In any case, surely there was something wrong with the plan. It would not have been enough to change the real situation. There was the illusion that in Bolivia he could count on the support of the Bolivian Communist Party that had initially helped embed them. There is the anecdote of Che who, on 1 January 1967, gathered his small guerrilla group and said: 'Well, the conditions under which this project was conceived are no longer the same because the Communist Party will not give the aid that was promised; therefore, those who came on the basis of the initial project are free, without disgrace, to leave.' We could say that it was at that moment the scenario of failure was more or less written.

I have already spoken about the influence of the Cuban Revolution, but I would like to correct the image a little today. In Latin America and perhaps beyond, there is the image of the original Cuban Revolution. Che remains a key figure, perhaps there is an iconic-religious excess. But at the same time, it can be interpreted differently. There is a political core to it, however, because he is one of the symbols of the twentieth century who has escaped corruption. He voluntarily extracted himself from a logic of bureaucratization. His own gesture may have failed in the end, but it also carries the symbolism of a permanent revolution that cannot stop in Cuba as soon as there is an opportunity, whether in the Congo, Haiti or Santo Domingo. The only chance for an island like Cuba, even more than for the USSR, is to open windows, to extend the revolution! So it is not just a romantic symbol, it also has real political content. Today I think that Che is being psychologized far too much: he was suicidal, he was this and that, he was even cruel, he executed a guy with his own hands. I think that, in the end, he deserves respect. They were infiltrated by a guy who was there to assassinate Fidel or Che. In the heat of a civil war rather than ordering a rank and file soldier to go and carry out an execution, he took on the responsibility. You can imagine it must not have been an easy decision to take.

This thread of revolutionary history, at least in Latin American, is not over.

9

17 January 1961: The murder of Patrice Lumumba

Belgium conceded independence to Congo in June 1960, but it intended to keep control of mining resources, particularly those in Katanga whose secession it supported. As Prime Minister of Congo, Patrice Lumumba tried to oppose this policy of plunder. Following Mobutu's coup d'état, the local authorities of Katanga assassinated Lumumba on the 17 January 1961. We remember the date of his assassination and of his supporters because it was to us emblematic of neo-colonialism. It is the organized plunder of wealth through the systematic support for armed groups on all sides, at the price of endless massacres. Moreover, the figure of Lumumba is intriguing. Sartre said that the death of Lumumba made him the whole of Africa and Césaire called him *'le Verbe'*. But Lumumba is almost unknown to young Western militants. I have the impression that we could see this as a symptom of a feeling of powerlessness in the face of the situation in Africa. We see only ethnic conflicts and an area for humanitarian intervention rather than for political solidarity because of a lack of knowledge as to whom to support and why.

It is true that Lumumba's image is rather blurred. I am not saying that other African independence activists, such as Amilcar Cabral[88] or leaders of the Angolan or Mozambican war of independence are very well known, but they are better known than Lumumba. There may be reasons for this. He was murdered young and I do not know if he left any writings because it is an oral culture. That does not mean that people did not write, but I think he did not write much. Maybe no more than Thomas Sankara did in Burkina Faso.

Lumumba's texts may not have been much read, if at all since we are in European culture, and they certainly would not have been as familiar to us as for example texts from the Latin American revolutionary movements. With the latter, we have the impression that despite the differences, we are talking about the same history and the same cultural heritage. For Africa, and this is a more obscure point, we are influenced by a colonial folkorization based on elements of reality. But this may be an unconscious or a defensive stance. The type of social development of African societies – not everywhere, for example South Africa – means that we are not spontaneously in the same framework. This is not to devalue it, but I have seen this with my African students much more than with Iranian students, for example. This reflects a different relationship to history, tradition, local cultures and languages. All this probably screens out a figure like Lumumba.

Yet I believe that the date is indeed symbolic for two reasons. First, at the time of African independence you could think there was a new beginning for the continent, even if it was a more nuanced process. Read René Dumont's book, *False Start in Africa*. Independence was a victory although there was still the task of building a society and a state. But what was immediately set in motion as mechanisms of subordination were neo-colonial policies of reconstruction or reconversion of the ties of economic dependence, of access to raw materials and of the mechanism of indebtedness – which came later. We can see this clearly in the case of the Congo. This entire strategy had been tried and tested by playing on the decomposition of the state apparatus. In the end there was state independence, but in most cases it did not lead to the construction of national realities. Unlike the formation of European states, where there was a to and fro between the nation and the state, a national reality does not clearly pre-exist. It is the state that creates a homogeneity and leads to a national reality.

It must be said that that in Africa, state independence was born out of the divisions of colonization, sometimes with ridiculous overlaps as for example with Tanzania. However, national realities could have been constructed, perhaps artificially, but that presupposed development, policies of redistribution and so on. But as these fragile plurinational states were emerging, imperialist plunder continued. Today this is reaching extreme forms, to the point where the interest payments on the debts of most Central African states are higher than their combined health and education budgets. This is not without consequences, particularly in terms of cultural re-colonization. When it is no longer possible to pay teachers, pre-recorded courses from multinational communication firms are broadcast instead, and tutors deliver programmes that are just ideological vehicles.

This was a laboratory that played very quickly on tribal realities that did not merge entirely into national entities. There were some extreme cases with obviously the major challenge of the Congo, but later there was Nigeria, or today but on a completely different scale, the Ivory Coast. It was also a question of playing on local wars and presenting them – which is the height of cynicism – as the resurfacing of a natural and inherent savagery to confirm the image of barbarity that is reflected back by those who are colonized. Most of these wars were ultimately instrumentalized or simply provoked by the interplay of interests and by the carving-up over and again of Africa. This has been a recurrent issue since the Berlin Congress at the end of the nineteenth century, the purpose of which was precisely the colonial carve-up of Africa.[89]

Lumumba's image does not need to be rehabilitated but to be enhanced. His importance stems from the fact that he is one of the first figures of African independence with an absolutely tragic destiny. At the time I was in the *Jeunesse Communiste* and we had no idea that Lumumba represented a communist movement. But just like Cuba or Algeria, Lumumba was part of the process, part of what we felt was a growing power. Learning that he had been murdered, that there was no corpse and that he had been dissolved in sulphuric acid, added tragedy to the circumstances of his death. It happened in a context where the emergence of the figure of Lumumba was also part of a whole.

Dates do matter. In 1961, the movements in the Portuguese colonies marked that whole period. Even if they were given particular attention after the explosion in Portugal of the 1970s, they already existed and were part of the rise of all these movements. There was in particular the cultural movement of *'négritude'* and of Caribbean literature. Caribbean in the broadest sense as there were major figures like Jacques Roumain in Haiti and Aimé Césaire.[90] There was also a very slight time lag with the emergence of the Black rights movement in the United States. The first riots in Los Angeles were not strictly Black riots but were the expression of a Black rights movement that was already present. In the student riots of 1961-62, which are less well known, there was also that expression. In this sense, the rise of the movement for Black rights in the United States and movement for independence in Africa are part of a whole.

We must also add the impact that Frantz Fanon, and especially his thought, had at the time.[91] This is surprising because today Fanon is one of the major reference points in colonial and post-colonial studies throughout the English-speaking world. In France, perhaps because of recent events, he is being rediscovered. But very little university research has been done in recent years around Fanon's thought. It is important because if we look at, and this is an arbitrary and partly symbolic choice, Fanon, Lumumba, and Malcolm X, and we could also add Cabral or the impact of the Cuban Revolution in the Caribbean, there is a whole sequence of the assertion of Black rights which grew out of predecessors such as W.E.B. Du Bois in the United States or C.L.R. Jameswho had discussions with Trotsky.[92] In France we only know of *The Black Jacobins* by C.L.R. James about the Haitian Revolution. It is *the* major book on the Haitian Revolution, written by a Black man, who was a Trotskyist, on the leadership of the Fourth International in 1939, and who was also a great specialist in the English-speaking press of cricket as a form of colonial relationship. James write a lot on cricket.

That was the background. It did not start from scratch in the United States. There was already a whole history of thinking on emancipation by the Black rights movement, which was re-energized by the rise of struggles for independence in Africa. And we have three symbolic figures – Fanon, Lumumba and Malcolm X – whose direction at that time illustrate what the dynamics of a black movement could be, that is to say a movement – we can read it in Fanon – that claimed its '*négritude*'. Besides, I think that at the time we cannot talk about pride, it came a little later in the 1960s. The history of pride, of shame, of being proud to be this or that ... No. We are proud of what we do, not of who we are!

We understand very well that this is a reaffirmation in the face of discrimination, and oppression. But for Fanon, Lumumba and Malcolm X, it is a demand that seeks convergence with the universal demands of the social movement and the labour movement, and that is what we are doing. And Fanon's texts, such as *Black Skin – White Masks*, are both a claim for '*négritude*' and at the same time he writes magnificent passages on the theme: 'My back is marked by the lashes of the whip, my face dripping with spittle ... but I do not want to let myself be anchored, mired in an origin, in an identity ... I'm part of a something that is coming.' All this is partly inspired by Sartre's philosophy.

Whereas today, on the contrary, identity crises turn towards a legitimacy of origins. The worst is in Jewish intellectual circles – including here in France – where the myth of the chosen people is being reactivated and where genocide is reinterpreted as a holocaust that becomes the negative proof of having been chosen. It is the confirmation by the genocide of a special status of the chosen people. And intelligent people like Jean-Claude Milner or Benny Levy are right in the middle of the mythology of origins and genealogy.[93] While all the leading figures of the liberation movements of the 1960s were claiming their particularity to be part of a universal future.

Malcolm X's personal trajectory is the very illustration of this. That is to say, going from the claim for Black rights linked to a religious claim (the Black Muslims) to the social question, which is probably what cost him his life. There is obviously a particular intelligence in the individual, but it is also because of his travels, his meeting with Che, and the encounters he made. This might seem anecdotal, but what I find interesting to remember is how his aspirations for liberation and his demands for recognition of an oppressed people and race, which were raised in the context of the colonial revolution, turn in a very general sense towards the workers' movement of the time. And the emblematic figures of all this are Che, Amilcar Cabral, Lumumba, etc. You have to see the comparison with today. Today, there is a new rise of struggles against neo-imperialism, against global war, against the re-colonization of the world, but the figures who have become symbolic internationally are Bin Laden, Zerkaoui, etc. And this broadly sums up the differences in context.

One last word: among the emblematic figures, I would add Ben Bella, with his limitations and qualities, and Ben Barka.[94] And since we are in France, it is never useless to recall Ben Barka and the fate that the French state, in collaboration with Moroccan royalty, had for him.

10

3 May 1968: The closing of the Sorbonne

On 3 May 1968, the Rector decided to close the Sorbonne. This date marked the beginning of the Paris May in a pivotal year for the workers' movement. However, these events were far from isolated and took place in an international context of struggle, both in the Western bloc and in the East. It was also a period of growth for extreme left-wing and libertarian currents. We need to go beyond the folkloric story that the current holders of power have made of it today, we must analyse this period: why did it happen then, what are its international origins and what are the contributions and consequences of May 68 for us today?

First of all, we must make a general very important point.

As the story is told by those in power, it often emphasizes certain facts and not others and, indeed, you yourself chose the date of 3 May and not 17 May, the beginning of the general strike. One event is linked to the other and it is therefore legitimate to speak of 3 May, but the accounts of May 68 have largely been by former students. We hear more from Cohn Bendit or others, including ourselves, on 1968, than from Georges Séguy's book on May from the workers' point of view for example.[95] It may have been read in the CGT, but that is not what is shown on the media.

The most important point I want to rectify today is how a mythology of 1968 was constructed.

As the anniversaries have come and gone, we have seen narratives of 1968 built up. There is one that was championed by Socialists in the 1980s as Mitterrand finally was elected – and Henri Weber is one of the makers of this narrative[96] – May 68 as the start of a cultural revolution or, as was said later, more of a change in society than a social revolution, a modernization of morals, a cultural *aggiornamento*, etc., which relativizes the general strike dimension.

If there had only been the student movement in May 68, it would have been interesting, but we would be talking about it in the same way as we talk about the Provos movement in Amsterdam in 1967 or the Berkeley students' movement in the 1960s or the SDS movement of German students in Berlin and its 'critical' university.[97]

If 1968 is a symbolic date in the world and not only about the French May, it is, I believe, first of all because it was the longest and most massive general strike in France's history. There are many interpretations. Was it the last of the heroic strikes of the nineteenth and twentieth centuries, was it the prefiguration of the social movements of the 21st century? Probably a little bit of both... It is a pivotal moment... where there is old and new. When footballers go into self-management, there is something new. It is a long time ago because these days they are far from being self-managed in successful clubs! The last person to call for self-management for footballers was Socrates, a great Brazilian player, a member of the Workers' Party at the time.[98] He was asked: 'What do you think of your coach?' 'My coach, I have the same relationship with him as I have with a boss. He's an exploiter, I'm an exploited man, well paid but still.'

On the one hand, the symbolic force of 1968 is the general strike, the most important features were the relatively new forms of democracy, protest, etc. that developed. On the other hand, 1968 became a world event, and experienced as such in France, because it echoed and resonated with a series of events taking place in the same year: the Prague Spring in Czechoslovakia until the Soviet intervention in August, the Tet offensive in Vietnam in February, which had just ended.[99] Then, although less spectacularly, the Olympic Games in Mexico City with Smith and Carlos's raised fists at the medal ceremony; and also the Tlatelolco massacre in Mexico, that is, the repression resulting in several hundred deaths in the Three Cultures Square on the eve of the Olympic Games.[100] There were also important student movements, including in Pakistan and then others, on a smaller scale in Poland. In fact, 1968 became the symbol of all this, that is to say of a particular context, but which was already reflected in the course of the movement.

Before 3 May, which was when it all kicked off, a few words on the movement that appeared, rightly or wrongly, as the detonator, that is the movement on the Nanterre campus, and in particular what happened on 22 March. Just before the Easter holidays, there was an open day of discussions in which, let us not exaggerate, there were perhaps 400-500 students. It was not bad for the time, but it was still a small minority, and the workshop discussions were on university reforms, anti-imperialist struggles, mainly Vietnam, and anti-bureaucratic struggles, mostly on Czechoslovakia and Poland. And the movement defined itself, unlike a student union, as a political-union movement. It was ephemeral, but we can clearly see the anti-capitalist, anti-bureaucratic and anti-imperialist sentiments. That was the seed at a time when it seemed that these different facets of resistance to oppression and exploitation were combined and could be linked.

Furthermore, it should also be added that the attempted assassination of Rudi Dutschke, the figurehead of the Berlin German student movement, also played a role in the development of the movement.[101] He was particularly present at the heart of a small militant minority in France, in particular the anarchists in Nanterre of the group of Duteuil and Cohn-Bendit or we in the JCR at the time, as Dutschke was perceived as our partner.[102] There too it was our history. We had met him at the end of January 1968 in Berlin, when we went to demonstrate at the great European demonstration on Vietnam. It was more or less the same culture. All the people of that time were coming out of that melting pot. Tariq Ali in England and so on.[103]

There was this movement of identification between the struggles.

Now there is a real question, though. Today, forty years or so later, we are not going to discuss it, because we do not have some sort of slide rule: was the situation pre-revolutionary? What is important is to emphasize what could have been done to go further, yes, to show that in any situation there are moments when we could have done something else, to see the moments when the movement was at crossroads, at a junction.

One crucial turning point was probably during the departure from De Gaulle to Baden-Baden and the meeting at Charlety, the meeting where they tried to relaunch Mendès France.[104]

Probably, there were other moments when the matter could have gone along a different path, when the first draft of the Grenelle agreements presented by Séguy in a general assembly to Renault was rejected, when he got booed.

I think it was rightly our role to insist on what could be done differently to go further. Does that mean social revolution was on the agenda?

In hindsight, we have some food for thought. All the same, compared to the scale of such a movement, the final compromise was relatively inexpensive for the bourgeoisie. The gains of 1968, while they are not negligible in terms of wages or union rights in the workplace, are far from having the symbolic and historical significance of the conquests of the Popular Front with paid holidays or of the Liberation with socialized health care. This was the result after the relationship of forces was very favourable in a period of growth with just around 200,000 unemployed. That is to say, what was called frictional unemployment at the time, fitting people's qualifications to the labour market, but not structural long-term unemployment as it is today. In a period without unemployment, the social weight of the workforce was obviously considerable.

So, the results were weak and the second problem that leads me to question the limits of 1968 is that this was a very strong movement, which occurred at the end of a phase of growth in a phase of relative prosperity – which does not mean that there were no poor people, of course. But in the end, it produced only minor differentiations in the labour movement. There was the emergence of the extreme left, which was new. Perhaps, following our exclusion from the PCF in 1966, we had, at the beginning of 1968, two or three hundred at the most. The Maoists a little more. Obviously, 1968 allowed these currents, which could have dissipated over time through discouragement, to develop. It was for us the confirmation that we were not completely zombies in our polemics with the PCF. Because the question at the time was: is revolution still conceivable in developed countries? That was the debate. Their answer was: the relative prosperity of the post-war boom means that revolutions are no longer on the agenda and that today we have to manage social compromise reasonably. We answered: 'No, we are still revolutionaries!' It was an act of faith or an act of reason, both. We saw from close up in 1968 that we were not dreaming, all the more so because behind 1968 there was the Italian Hot Autumn, there was the contagion effect in Europe, etc.[105] We were not dreaming.

So that was important, but while a radical left survived, which pulled itself out or freed itself from the grip of the traditional union and political apparatuses, there was lesser immediate, deep-going effect than in 1947, at the time of the Renault strikes led in part by *Lutte Ouvrière*, or even, in 1936, with the appearance of Pivertism.[106] The effects were very limited, there was one: the collapse of social democracy corrupted or compromised in the Algerian war, but the PCF extricated itself well enough.

In the 1969 presidential elections its candidate Duclos received 22 per cent of the vote and the Socialist Party with Defferre and Mendès France as a ticket got 5 per cent.[107]

If it really was such a mature movement from a revolutionary point of view, it could still have been beaten or channelled by bureaucrats, but there would have been more differentiation in the labour movement. I think that the limit of what came out of it perhaps indicates, in hindsight, the limits of the movement itself. On the other hand, there were trade union effects, notably through a strengthening of the CFDT, which was not the CFDT of Chérèque or Nicole Notat.[108] There was a real left in the CFDT at that time with, for example, someone like Frédo Krumnow in the textile sector who was perhaps not a revolutionary but who learnt the lesson of self-management from the 1968 events.[109] Yes, that was something but in part rather shows the limits.

So today we have two ways of looking at the events.

One that reduces 1968 in retrospect to a great student movement of cultural modernization. This has been the line of many of those 1968 veterans who have found a new home in social democracy.

Another thing is the discourse of Finkielkraut and his consorts, or Luc Ferry, who speak bluntly of 'the fault of 68'. The fault of 1968 is the beginning of the decomposition, the loosening of morals, the loss of the taste for work... so a kind of libertarian liberalization of morals which at the same time produces social disintegration. Today it has even become perhaps dominant in relation to the previous discourse – they talk of the need for a return to order and try and squeeze the life out of all that may have remained or been inherited from 1968. This is the business of Sarkozy or others today.

As for me, the commemorations are psychologically understandable the older one gets. Ten years from 1968 in 1978, twenty years in 1988, now thirty years, it is becoming trying but, at the same time, I think there is still a small fight to be had over its meaning. We have to challenge these dominant narratives of 1968 with its 'reading' of the stakes involved in France and internationally, which have now become 'officialized' ideologically.

11

26 August 1970: In memory of the wife of the Unknown Soldier

On 26 August 1970, nine women laid a wreath at the Arc de Triomphe in memory of the wife of the unknown soldier. There is somebody even more nameless than the unknown soldier: his wife. This act marked the birth of the feminist movement in France, in the 1970s, because in the history of the workers' movement there had been a difficulty inherent to militant combat in distinguishing the place of women inside the movements. Until 1968 women were present in the demonstrations but the spokespersons were often essentially men, and in fact it was precisely after this period of upheaval emerging from 1968 that the discourse of women was able to take on an autonomous form in relation, exactly, to the party and union leaderships which had to some degree lost credibility through the experience of 1968. This feminist movement marked a significant evolution in the history of activism and the question which I would like to ask is: 'What in your view is the influence and importance of this movement now, but also perhaps what are the limits to which activism leads when it is marked by a Marxism which has always, perhaps a little too much, considered the question of capitalist exploitation as a significant thing in relation to more secondary issues?'

Yes, if we need a symbolic date of birth, we can take 26 August 1970 as a reference point, that is what is remembered now. But for the feminist movement as for other movements, there is no absolute date of birth. If the movement appeared, or if it crystallized symbolically around this laying of the wreath at the Arc de Triomphe, fermentation existed in the preceding years. Although women were not seen much on the platforms or leading demonstrations in 1968 – this has been stressed during this anniversary year of 1968 – if we look a bit further, we can certainly see that there was something brewing, coming to the surface. For example, in the film by Chris Marker *À bientôt, j'espère* on the strikes at Rhodiaceta, or that of the watchmakers in Besançon before 1968, we see precisely the appearance of women.[110] This was filmed before 1968. They demanded their place within trades unionism and in the union struggle and highlighted all the contradictions of the organization of their daily life and their domestic tasks. So, there was something there, already, we can see in France and even more so at the international scale, inasmuch as the traditions and cultures of the feminist movement are quite differentiated according to the history of the countries. There is a less discontinuous history of British and US feminism than is the case with feminism in France. In the 1960s there was already a feminist movement in the USA and in Britain which can be found in the two issues of the review *Partisans*, which must have been published in 1970 and 1971, two special issues on feminism which had a foundational value. If my memory is correct, two thirds of them were made up of translation of texts, notably from the US or British feminist movements.[111]

As for France, in fact, we can speak of a birth reflecting two groundswells, two fundamental movements in society. On the one hand, the massive entry of the women workers into the modern workforce, which is one of the consequences of the years of growth and notably of the development of new service sectors. On the other hand, or parallel to this, and this is coherent, there were also increased levels of co-education in higher education. Which was also, even if this has sometimes been exaggerated, among the root causes of the struggles in Nanterre, inasmuch as we can easily remember that the mobilization against single-sex halls of residence was one of the preludes to the Nanterre student movement.

As an anecdote, and it is still worth remembering, I joined the *Jeunesses Communistes* in 1962 at the time of the Charonne demonstrations. I was in a mixed high school and, paradoxically, when you joined the *Jeunesses* there were two distinct circles: a circle of boys of the *Jeunesses Communistes*, and a circle of girls called the UJFF, *l'Union des Jeunes Filles de France*. This felt a bit like a Catholic private school and there was something of that about it, with an underlying moralism, which was the heritage of Jeannette Vermeersch, the familial and natalist policy which the Communist Party had.[112] So, these questions were being raised at the time.

The date that we remember as the pivotal date was a birth and also a rebirth.

It tends to be forgotten that there were feminist movements in France and notably in the nineteenth century at the time of Flora Tristan and Louise Michel, and that they were fairly powerful.[113] For example, it is too little known, and I will come back to this in relation to the Marxist heritage on the 'woman question' or feminism, that the rebirth of the workers' movement in France after the great defeat of June 1848 was marked to a great extent, if we look at the 1860s, by meetings in the Parisian neighbourhoods which did not focus on social demands such as wages, but were around the themes of family, marriage and divorce. Basically, the reconstruction of a social movement before the Paris Commune was to a considerable extent achieved around these themes, with an obvious confrontation with the moral, religious, familial order and so on.

Thus, all this has been a little lost. Its continuity was broken notably because of the effects, not only in the Soviet Union, of the wave, you might say the diffusion, I would put it like that, of what Trotsky called in one of the chapters of *The Revolution Betrayed* : 'Thermidor in the Family'.[114]

A rupture with what had been done in the area of women's liberation, without being perfect, in the early years of the Russian Revolution. It should be remembered however that this went as far as the abolition of incest at a time when Freud was not widely read, and divorce by simple registration. Not without contradiction, since in a society where relations of sex remained inegalitarian, divorce by simple registration was often reflected by repudiations and armadas of abandoned children. They had to go into reverse gear. But there was in any case an intention which was strongly marked and quite audacious in relation to the *mores* of the time, which regressed following the re-establishment on the contrary of all forms of authority, in state, party and family. That is the meaning of 'The Thermidor in the Family' which was also reflected by new legislation on the family and on inheritance in the 1930s. And this was spread internationally by the Communist parties, notably in France. I have just evoked the symbolic figure of Jeannette Vermeersch, who was the companion of PCF general secretary Maurice Thorez and who was a genuine militant for the familial order, making the Party, the dominant force in the workers' movement at the time, a veritable bastion of the moral and familial order.

We can say that this vice began to loosen before 1968, which was a formidable accelerator, and we saw the emergence of this feminist movement. Now, starting from the symbolic date of 26 August 1970, I think that would be interesting to look back, with the hindsight that we have today, on the fact that, initially, as with other social phenomena of the period moreover, there was a relatively close relationship between the rising power of the social movement – the workers' movement, trade unions and so on – and this women's movement. There was a sort of convergence or a fairly natural alliance between social and feminist themes. For example, we remember a historic report – this was practically a cultural revolution in the CGT – by Jean-Louis Moynot, at the time confederal secretary – that would be in 1972 or 1973 – which took note of the consequences of the growth of the female salariat.

Parallel to this, but in a combined manner – and I would not wish to embellish it in hindsight – we had the eruption of themes like violence against women, the right to choose, themes which today we would characterise as societal, and which at the time were closely inter-related. This also contributed to the rise of women's groups, of the different women's reviews which appeared. If we leaf through today what was then the feminist press: the publications of Remue-ménage, the Flora Tristan circles, *Le torchon brûle* then, a little later the *Cahiers du féminisme*.[115] These were publications which closely linked the specific demands of women with the social movement or what was called at the time the workers' movement.

And I think that which, at the time, was closely linked has become disconnected like the rest. In their book *The New Spirit of Capitalism* the sociologists Luc Boltanski and Ève Chiapello speak of the artistic critique and the social critique of society. They understand by social critique that which relates to demands around wages, employment, living conditions and by artistic critique that which relates more to everyday life and to forms of alienation.

All this was strongly linked, I think also that it was perhaps one of the great campaigns of these 1970s. We remember the vote on the Veil law but, well, it was only one link in a genuine mobilization. It was a legislative battle which should not be minimized, but which could take place because of all the mobilizations there had been beforehand. First the manifesto on the right to abortion, then trials like that in Bobigny which made history.[116] And then, throughout the second half of the 1970s – which has moreover been the subject of an important debate on what type of campaign could be waged – a real democratic campaign was waged by the MLAC (Movement for the Liberation of Abortion and Contraception), which was a mixed single-theme campaign, and which culminated, I think, in the biggest demonstration on these themes which was in 1979.[117] But it was at that time that we began to finally see the divergence of this close inter-relationship between what I would call generalist social demands and the specific demands of women, with a tendency incarnated notably, moreover, by what was known as *Psych et Po* and which gave rise to the Éditions des femmes, led principally by Antoinette Fouque.[118] Finally, the two questions became delinked and this was reflected by the position of *Psych et Po* – which in my opinion says more about it than the theoretical debates – on the presidential election of 1981 which was to support Mitterrand from the first round while saying that, finally, parties being masculine by definition, one could vote for them as a stage and lesser evil, but there was no overall alternative strategy to these parties.

There was a radicalism, notably on the questions of violence in everyday life, of the body, of the feminist movement but which began finally to delink from the social demands at the very time when the implementation of austerity policies in Europe posed, from a certain viewpoint, major social problems specific to women, even if they do not have the exclusivity of them. The deterioration of various social services, of crèches, quite simply worsened everyday life. The rise in unemployment, even if it was not reflected, like other periods, by a total expulsion of women from the world of work, was reflected by increased precarity or a maintenance of inequalities in relation to employment, wages and so on.

Thus, we have seen this kind of delinking of the movement which marks, I think, as for the rest, a turning point on the threshold of the 1980s of the women's movement as it existed in the 1970s. It has not gone away.

So this is the other problem. That which tends to be a little less visible, let us put this in a general formula, is the organized activist wing of the women's movement. Now the social effects are very much present, that is the profound effects of things which are no longer accepted or acceptable or which have changed profoundly. Nothing is irreversible and nothing is ever won definitively for women, no more than it can be for men, but there are deep-lying effects which continue to work through. In the trade union organizations and the political parties on the other hand, we have seen, I believe, a massacre of the publications that I have just cited which have more or less disappeared one after another.

But, nonetheless, socially the movement subsists. So, then, what remains of it today, there also I believe it is difficult to define because there are obviously gains to defend, inasmuch as they are periodically challenged, on the right to abortion or on a series of rights or in particular for immigrant women and so on. But let us say that there is a heritage, a culture, there again a memory finally of the women's movement which has percolated, as some would say, that is it has spread profoundly within society and it is more difficult to reverse. Is the law on parity an illustration of this? To some extent, but it is also the illustration of a setback: that is that a law was needed to impose it. Personally, I say it frankly, I did not sign the first appeal on this. I was quite perplexed because it was nevertheless introducing a biological difference in the political field. Good, now, if it is a point of support, some have moreover presented it as temporary point of support, to force a closer approximation of parity, but which effectively in any case appears to me more just, if we wish to take a voluntarist measure, than quotas. Because the sole quota conceivable in this case is an equality which corresponds to a de facto equality, whereas with quotas there are no criteria to calculate what the correct proportion would be.

Now, how does this relate to Marxism... It is true that the feminist movement in its activist form has contributed to posing a problem which is not completely new, we should not exaggerate, but on which all the same today the culture of the social movements, of the radical left has evolved. Not to hierarchize a series of dominations, not to say: 'There is a principal contradiction and there are secondary contradictions', but to consider that all human beings are multiple and that they are then subject, with different levels of intensity according to the moments of their lives, to oppression and exploitation at work, sexual or gender oppression in the family, or at work also, or in everyday life, an oppression which can be racial or ethnic, and many others also.

So you have a combination, a bouquet, a sheaf finally of forms of resistance to various oppressions. On the other hand, the real debate, for example with the sociologists of the Bourdieu school, is on whether all these oppressions have exactly the same function in our society. Personally, I tend to believe, to think that there are two of them that do not exactly play the same role and around which quite a few things nonetheless are structured: the relationship of social exploitation and the relationship of gender domination. This goes back a long way – besides, nothing says that by eradicating the conditions of exploitation we would eradicate the evolution of the psyche – in terms of what could be called *mores*, which do not march to the rhythm of parliamentary legislations. That is why we decided on the necessity, which we maintain today, of an autonomous women's movement, inasmuch as nothing suggests that ending capitalism would mechanically, automatically, end the oppression of women.

So there is a more articulated thought today on how these different forms of resistance or mobilization against forms of domination which are not reducible to each other can converge and around what themes. I think this would be an extrapolation but a notion like that of hegemony, taken principally but not only from Gramsci – well, that is what we generally have in mind – aids thinking on how these different grievances in relation to the dominant society can articulate with each other to develop an overall counter-culture.[119]

Then, now, a final word perhaps on the Marxist heritage here. It is not so outmoded as is often thought. Sure, I would not say that Marx was a great pioneer of feminism. At least in his everyday life he was fairly conformist, let us say, in relation to his daughters or to his married life. Engels, very much less so, and from this viewpoint it is not by chance that Engels was all the same, in a certain fashion, a pioneer, even if today we can discuss in the light of studies not available to him at the time the theses defended in *The Origin of the Family, Private Property and the State*.[120] He at least aligned his everyday life with a non-conformist thought, whether on death or on the family, inasmuch as he was living 'over the brush', in the language employed at the time, with a working-class Irish woman, which was doubly scandalous in polite Mancunian society.[121] But more profoundly, beyond anecdotes, Marx himself considered the condition of women. It can be said that there was a discrepancy between his discourse and then... well you can say that being an enlightened male chauvinist is already a form of progress, and not claim that he was totally revolutionary in his head!

But, for example, and for me it is one of the three criteria of what real progress would be: not quantitative progress of how many tons of steel or coal, and so on, but the massive reduction of working time, thus the reduction of the time of forced working time, all that which finally singularizes the needs of individuals and which makes of each individual a unique being and precisely the transformation, I would say the transformation, no more, of the relationship between the sexes, between the genders, as we put it today. Because this, he says it explicitly: the relation between man and woman, it is the first experience and finally the most revealing of the relationship to difference, of the relationship to someone different. Hence finally, in a world where there is an inferiority of women, there will also be a discrimination against the immigrant, the foreigner and so on. This was notably in his youthful texts. Well, after that, we have to follow the ups and the downs, the best and the worst of the workers' movement, for which Marx is not always responsible.

12

11 September 1973: The fall of Allende

On 11 September 1973, the Chilean military put a bloody end to the three year reformist experience of the Salvador Allende government.[122] Augusto Pinochet continued a new cycle of bloody repression and brutal economic liberalism that had started in Bolivia.[123] He was soon followed by other dictatorships in South America. In 1979, in another context, the Sandinistas brought some hope by taking power in tiny Nicaragua.[124] Ten years later, in 1990, strangled by the American blockade, they lost power through a general election.

The United States, which intervenes throughout South America, has no intention of allowing the people in its backyard to raise their heads against its interests. The two experiences of Chile and Nicaragua took place in very different contexts. On the one hand, Salvador Allende elected by Congress, on the other, an armed seizure of power by the Sandinistas. They raise the question of state power and above all how to retain it, with whom and why.

As a subsidiary question, I would also like to examine the place given, or rather the lack of place given, to indigenous or assimilated peoples in these processes.

Perhaps we should begin by recalling that 11 September – in 1973 not that of 2001 – was first and foremost an emotional shock. We were transfixed by the news that arrived on the radio from the headquarters of the Presidential Palace, La Moneda, and then by the announcements that gradually came in about the success of the coup d'état. At first we hoped it would not succeed, since another coup d'etat had failed in June three months before, but then we got the news of Allende's death and so on.

How can such an emotional shock be explained, this had not been our reaction during the bigger bloodbath in 1965 when the Indonesian Communist Party was crushed or more recently with the repression of the Sudanese Communist Party?[125] I believe it is because there was a very strong identification in Europe and Latin America with what was happening in Chile. There was a feeling that this was indeed a new scenario and a possibility, practically a laboratory experiment, which was valid for both Europe and Latin America, in different ways.

So, why was it so important for Europe?

Because we had the impression, partly false I would say today, that we finally had a country that was a reflection of our own reality. Unlike other Latin American countries, there was a strong communist party, there was a socialist party represented or led by Salvador Allende, there was an extreme left of the same generation as ours, small groups like MAPU, and MIR born in 1964-65 under the impulse of the Cuban Revolution.[126] There was an identification with the latter organization, with its militants, with its leaders who were practically of our generation, who had a fairly comparable background. The MIR was formed from two sources: on the one hand inspired by Che Guevara and the Cuban Revolution; on the other hand there was a Trotskyist influence, it must be said, through a great historian of Latin America, Luis Vitale.[127] He was one of the founding fathers of the MIR, even if he was removed from it or left shortly afterwards. All this in a country where, in the end, Stalinism had never been dominant, including on the left, nor did it have the role that the communist party had in Argentina, for example.

There was a specific factor in Chile, which is one of the difficulties in understanding the situation. The Chilean Socialist Party, even though it called itself socialist, had little to do with European social democracy. It was a party that had been built in the 1930s as a reaction, in opposition to the Stalinization of the Communist International. So it was a party more to the left of the CP than to the right, so there was a strong sense given to the idea that Chile could give the example of a scenario where the left came to power through elections. This would then be the beginning of a social process of radicalization leading to, or, let us say, transitioning towards a radical social revolution at a time when, it should also be remembered, the prestige of the Cuban Revolution in Latin America was, if not intact, then at least still very important.

I believe there are still lessons for us about what happened in Chile.

Today, I would be more cautious about this reflection of European realities. I think that, seen from a distance, there was a tendency to underestimate the social relations and the reserves of reaction and conservatism that existed in Chilean society. We saw them a lot in the army because, as was said and repeated at the time, the army had been trained by German instructors on the Prussian army model, which was already not very encouraging. But what is more, as I have seen since then, it is a country where the Catholic tradition, the conservative Catholic current, is important.

And besides, this was just a starting point. Allende was elected in September-October 1970, in a presidential election, but only with a relative majority of about 37 per cent. For his nomination to be ratified by the Assembly conditions were set. These conditions included two key aspects: no interference with the army and respect for private property. These were the two limits set from the outset by the dominant classes, by the institutions, for accepting Allende's investiture.

Nevertheless, it is true that the electoral victory raised people's hopes and sparked a strengthening of the social movements, which culminated in a major electoral victory in the municipal elections of January 1971. I believe that Popular Unity, the left-wing coalition on which Allende was relying at that time, had on this occasion (and only then) an absolute majority in an election.

This obviously gave greater legitimacy to developing the process. So we had an electoral victory, a radicalization, but also a polarization that was initially internal to Chile, which gradually translated into a mobilization of the right, including action on the streets. The landmark date was the lorry drivers' strike in October 1972.[128] But it should not be thought that it was employee-led: it was the employers who organized it. Chile's long geographical configuration meant that road transport was strategic. So there was this truckers' strike, therefore, supported by what were called *cacerolazos*[129], i.e. protest movements, particularly by middle-class consumers in Santiago – Santiago makes up more than half of the country in terms of population. It constituted a first attempt at destabilization in the autumn of 1972. Autumn for us of course, it was Spring there. The seasons have to be reversed.

At that point, there was finally a debate on the way forward for the Chilean process, which opened up two possibilities in response to the destabilization of the right. The latter was also strongly supported by the United States. We know today with the disclosures of the Condor plan how much and for how long the United States had been involved in the preparation of the coup d'état, through the multinationals but also through American military advisers. So in early 1973, after the warning signal of the lorry drivers' strike, there were several options. Either a radicalization of the process, with increased incursions into the private property sector, with radical redistribution measures, wage increases, and so on, all of which were debated. Or on the contrary, and this was the thesis that prevailed, put forward by Vukovik, Minister of Economy and Finance, a member of the Communist Party, to reassure the bourgeoisie and the ruling classes by definitively delimiting the area of public property or social property, and by giving additional guarantees to the military.

We are not going to give a detailed history, but what were the key events?

The second episode of destabilization was much more dramatic, no longer a corporate strike like that of the lorry drivers, but in June 1973 we saw a first attempt, a dry run for a coup d'état, the so-called *tankazo*, in which the army, in fact a tank regiment, took to the streets but was neutralized.

I believe that this was the crucial moment when the debate took place. For example, it was the moment when the MIR, which was a small organization of a few thousand very dynamic militants – we must not overestimate its size, but for Chile it was significant – proposed joining the government, but under certain conditions. After the failure of the first coup d'état, the question arose of forming a government whose centre of gravity would shift to the left, which would take measures to punish or disarm the conspiring military. But what was done was exactly the opposite.

That is to say, between the period of June 1973 and the actual coup d'état of 11 September 1973, there was repression against the movement of soldiers in the barracks, searches to disarm the militants who had accumulated arms in anticipation of resistance to a coup d'état, and then, above all, additional pledges given to the army with the appointment of generals to ministerial posts, including Augusto Pinochet, the future dictator.

So there was a momentum shift, and Miguel Enriquez, the secretary general of the MIR who was assassinated in October 1974, a year later, wrote a text, in this intermediate period between the dry run and the coup d'état, which was called 'When were we the strongest?' I think he was extremely lucid: up to August 1973 there were demonstrations by 700,000 demonstrators in Santiago, supporting Allende and responding to the coup d'état. That was indeed the moment when a counteroffensive by the popular movement was possible. On the contrary, the response was a shift to the right of the government alliances and additional pledges given to the military and ruling classes, which in reality meant in the end encouraging the coup d'état.

That is how we were surprised. You referred to the reformism of Salvador Allende but, in the end, compared to our reformists, he was still a giant of the class struggle. If we look at the archive documents today, he still has to be respected.

In the Chile solidarity movement, which was very important in the years that followed, 1973, 1974 and 1975, I would say that we were somewhat sectarian about Allende, who was made into someone responsible for the disaster. That does not change the political problem. It implies respect for the individual, but there is still a conundrum: during the first hours of the coup d'état, he still had national radio, it was still possible to call for a general strike, whereas a call was made in the end for static resistance in the workplaces, and so on. Perhaps it was not possible. Even an organization like the MIR, which was supposed to be prepared militarily, was caught off guard by the coup. We see this today in Carmen Castillo's book, *An October Day in Santiago* or in her film.[130] They were caught off guard perhaps, in my opinion, because they did not imagine such a brutal and massive coup d'état. They imagined the possibility of a coup d'état, but one that would be, in a way, half-baked that would usher in a new period of virtual civil war, with hotbeds of armed resistance in the countryside. Hence the importance they had given – and this is related to the other aspect of the question – to working among the peasants of the Mapuche minority, particularly in the south of the country.

But the coup d'état was a real sledgehammer blow. They had not really prepared, or even probably envisaged, a scenario of bringing together the organs of popular power that did exist; the so-called 'industrial belt committees' (*cordones*) that were more or less developed forms of self-organization, mainly in the suburbs of Santiago; the 'communal commandos' in the countryside; work in the army; and finally even in Valparaíso an embryo of a popular assembly, a kind of local soviet. Whatever else can be said, all that existed and suggests what could have been possible – but that would have required the will and the strategy. It was another way to respond to the coup d'état, whether in June or September, with a general strike, disarming the army, something akin to an insurrection. It was always risky, but you have to weigh it up against the price of the coup d'état in terms first of all of human lives, of the disappeared, of the tortured. Above all, you have to consider the price in terms of peoples' living conditions, when we see what Chile is today, after more than thirty years of Pinochet's dictatorship. It has been a laboratory for neoliberal policies. It was a historic defeat. If you look at two neighbouring countries, Chile and Argentina, the social movement in Argentina has quickly recovered its fighting spirit after the years of dictatorship, despite the thirty thousand people who disappeared.[131] In Chile, the defeat is clearly of a different scope and duration.

Nicaragua, actually, happened in a different period altogether.

I believe that the coup d'état in Chile was the epilogue of the revolutionary ferment that followed the Cuban Revolution for 10-15 years in Latin America. And as you pointed out in the introduction, the dates clearly tell the story: three months before the coup d'état in Chile, I think it was June 1973, there was the coup d'état in Uruguay. In 1971 there was the coup d'état in Bolivia. While the dictatorship had fallen in Argentina, it returned in 1976. But let us say that symbolically, the killing of Allende, the disappearance of Enriquez and practically the entire leadership of the MIR, closed the cycle initiated by the Cuban Revolution, the OLAS conference[132], and Che's expedition to Bolivia in 1966.

Nicaragua, finally, was perhaps the inauguration of another cycle, or a starting point that was somewhat of a shock. I was talking earlier about Luis Vitale. He had surprised us at a meeting in 1976 when we were taking stock of this regression in Latin America, saying: 'Yes, but the epicentre – that was the formula used – the epicentre has shifted, the next move is Nicaragua.' Frankly, many of us did not know where Nicaragua was in 1976. I do not want to say that Vitale was a prophet or a wizard, but he did see something coming in Central America, with its 'weak link' dictatorships, in very particular conditions with poorly-organized societies. The Chilean dictatorship had a social base. These dictatorships, Somoza and the like, were quite different, they were based on little.[133] This explains why the Sandinista Front was an organization that was almost nothing in 1967, since after the repression and failure of a guerrilla movement in the Pancasan region, it was reduced to fewer than a hundred militants.[134] We worked with them at the time, they asked for help in training from the Palestinians. Here we have the opposite process to Chile, first a victory of a people's insurrectional or military movement, I will not go into the three strategic lines that cohabited in the Sandinista Front. In the end they managed to combine, which was not a foregone conclusion: an extended popular war line in the countryside represented by Tomàs Borge, a more insurrectional line promoted by Jaime Wheelock, and then the Ortega brothers, which represented yet another third variant.[135] But in the end all this was combined in this specific context. It was the political and military victory of 1979 that inaugurated an electoral process.

What was new about the Nicaraguan affair was that the leadership of a revolution, or of the first victorious stage of a revolution, agreed to submit to the test of electoral legitimacy. It can be said that it was an impossible gamble, in a small country with less than three million inhabitants. When we talk about the working class, for example, in Nicaragua, we have to have the figures in mind: 27 thousand employees in companies with more than 100 employees, mainly woodworking companies, bottling companies for sparkling water. We still need to know what we are talking about. The agrarian issue was fundamental, and perhaps the indigenous issue, I will come back to that.

The problem, to get to the heart of the matter, is that Nicaragua was defeated a long time before it was defeated in the elections, which meant that the so-called 'low-intensity' war – the expression is almost ironic – financed by the United States very openly, forced an already very impoverished country to devote fifty per cent of its budget to defence, and to impose conscription in a country where that was not the tradition. It was very unpopular in the countryside, people were not used to sons going into the military. The war effort was a great social and moral drain on the country. As long as there was a possibility, and it was a real one, of extending the Nicaraguan revolution to Central America, it could hold out. And the possibility existed, especially in El Salvador, where there were several attempts at insurrection that were on the verge of winning.[136]

But the turning point, I think, was Guatemala. On Guatemala, we can read the testimony of someone who is now dead, Mario Payeras, one of the founders of the Guerrilla Army of the Poor (*Ejército Guerrillero de los Pobres* or EGP).[137] He explained to us, including orally, how paradoxically the Nicaraguan Revolution became a negative factor for the Guatemalan Revolution. In what sense? Quite simply because they thought they were dealing with dictators of the Somoza type, but they were facing military advisers. In 1984 there was a march on Guatemala City: the people were faced with Taiwanese and Israeli military advisers, specialists in counter-insurgency. They were no longer an army of thugs, *tontons macoutes* or something like that, they were really professionals in international civil war, one could almost say. As a result, Guatemala and El Salvador lost, and from that point on, the electoral defeat of the Sandinistas was, I am not saying inevitable in 1989-90, but it had, through attrition, become a likely outcome.

What can be discussed about the Sandinistas' politics, from my point of view, is not so much the fact of having carried out the elections, because holding on against all odds could have been worse, but the fact that they did not try and maintain a twofold source of legitimacy.

For a while there was what was called the Council of State. We must not imagine that it was like the *Conseil d'état* in France. It was an assembly where there were the employers' organizations, including Violetta Chamorro etc., and where there were just about all the social movements.[138] It was a kind of people's chamber whose legitimacy to defend the gains of agrarian reform and a whole series of things could have been used against the elected parliamentary assembly. So maintaining a dual legitimacy for a while, that was conceivable. Furthermore, we must not ignore what was discovered later on, which is the extreme rapidity – which must be a lesson in poor or very poor countries like this one – of the explosion of corruption, including among the Sandinistas. This is what has been called the *Piñata*, at the highest level of the Sandinista leadership. At the end of the day the strongest ideological convictions are not insensitive to the material logic of the world. This has also been an element in the Sandinista government's loss of moral credibility.

There is a pattern to the dates: the year 1989, as we can see in hindsight, also closes another cycle of about ten years. 1989 saw the Ochoa trial in Cuba and five years later the failure of Lula's second candidacy in 1994 in Brazil, at a time when Lula had not yet been restyled 'to be a presentable and eligible candidate'. He came very, very close to an electoral victory that would have produced a whole new political context. It was also the fall of the Berlin Wall, etc. So something changes in 1989-90, of which Nicaragua is a part.

Regarding indigenous politics... In Chile, I believe there had been a real effort and a willingness by extreme left-wing organizations to address the issue. In Nicaragua, it was more complicated with the problem of the Miskitos and Bluefields.[139] There, perhaps the Sandinistas, by not dealing specifically with the indigenous people of the Bluefields coast and by not providing specific answers, opened the door to their manipulation because, without being paranoid, there was a whole apparatus of ethnologists in the CIA which manipulated ethnic issues, and that played a role.

13

10 May 1981: The election of François Mitterrand

On 10 May 1981 François Mitterrand was elected. On 3 May 1979, Margaret Thatcher had been elected Prime Minister of the United Kingdom as leader of the Conservative Party. Eight months after that, on 20 January 1981, Ronald Reagan began his first term as President of the United States by declaring: 'Government is not the solution to our problem, government is the problem.'

Working people found out very quickly that this had nothing to do with Bakunin. The implementation of a liberal doctrine and the desire to destroy the trade unions would soon be put into effect in both countries. On 5 August 1981, 11 359 striking air traffic controllers were dismissed overnight by Ronald Reagan.[140] After months of strike action, Margaret Thatcher gave nothing to the British miners.[141] In foreign affairs, these two elections resulted in a increased series of military interventions. In France, nothing of the sort since, on 10 May 1981, the left, which had participated in May 1968 thirteen years earlier, finally came to power. The workers now knew that they could count on Bernard Tapie, Laurent Fabius and Jack

Lang[142] to implement their demands. Did not the decade ahead look bright for the labour movement?

Bright ? Certainly there had been tremendous illusions in this new government.

On the evening of 10 May 1981 – I was not in Paris, I had escaped – drenched by the storm at the Bastille, people were shouting 'Mitterrand, du soleil' (Mitterrand, bring us sunny days). So we were indeed waiting for a decade or a seven-year period of the sunlit uplands. That was not exactly what happened.

I think it is important to include the date and the sequence that follows, at least that of the 1980s and of Mitterrand's first term of office (without going as far as his second term) within a historical movement or a broader historical period.

Because, actually, Mitterrand had more or less announced his political strategy in 1968 in a very, very clear way if you read the texts of the time or if you read his thinking in a little book published in 1971 called *Ma part de vérité* (My truth). He explained very clearly that, in 1968 and during the four days of critical crisis in the regime, that is, during de Gaulle's departure from Baden-Baden, when he called for a people's government – that was the formula chosen – to fill the huge void that was opening up, he intended that this government should be, in his words, without exclusivity and without a rigid composition. In other words, a government open to partners from the centre, even from the right. He too had the idea of opening up long before Sarkozy, but in the opposite direction. And he tried, to a certain extent, to carry this out in 1981 with the entry of Michel Jobert, a historic Gaullist or a few others in the government. Without rigidity meant, in particular, not only that he would accept but that he wanted the participation of communist ministers, but in a homeopathic amount that did not excessively colour the government. In fact, if we look at it, in 1981 he chose four communist ministers, but he gave them Health, Vocational Training, Transport and the Civil Service. So, in none of the strategic departments, let us put it that way.

In other words, it was his project and he succeeded.

It should be remembered that the Socialist Party only won 5.5 per cent in the 1969 presidential election for the Defferre/Mendès-France ticket. In other words, what Mitterrand did was a genuine transformation of the political relationship of forces. He laid it out very clearly in his writings. It was a question of reconstructing this relationship through the prolonged alliance of the Union of the Left and the Common Programme with the Communist Party. In this way he was able to reverse the balance of power in the left to the detriment of the PCF. This he did in a very coherent and consistent way, in the 1968 proposal, but again in the way he reacted after there was disunity of the left.

Remember also that in 1978 it seemed that the left was going to win the parliamentary elections. In any case, the polls indicated this as possible. Then, in the year preceding the election, which was to be in March or April 1978, we had the controversy, the disunity, initiated in particular by the PCF, which meant that these legislative elections were lost.[143] Some concluded that a complete change of strategy was needed on the left, abandoning the project of a Union of the Left. This was, in fact, the position adopted impetuously by Michel Rocard at the 1979 Socialist congress in Metz. I am not mentioning this for the sake of detail, but to show to what extent Mitterrand really followed a political line. At the Metz congress, he maintained, despite the bad will, the negative attitude of the PCF, a line of union on the left. He was convinced he would not achieve his aim of transforming the whole left in France unless there was an electoral victory and the inclusion of the PCF in the coalition government. In the end he won the Metz SP congress.

So, for him, 1981 was a godsend. Because, if he was indeed obliged to say something in 1968, I believe that the idea of getting into government on the backs of a general strike of nearly ten million strikers did not particularly attract him. In 1978, an election victory in a general election was probably not the best scenario for him either. I think the fundamental point is that in 1978 the momentum of 1968 was not totally exhausted. It had definitely lost a lot of momentum. I am not just saying in France, but from a European perspective.

Let us say that, with the beginning of the economic crisis in 1973-74, the economic downturn, the halt to the Portuguese Revolution in November 1975, the monarchical transition in Spain, the turn to austerity in Italy, also in 1976, in the name of historical compromise, we can say that the hypothesis of an electoral victory of the left in 1978 in France was the last possible reflex of the post-1968 period.[144]

Finally, I believe that for Mitterrand the scenario of a presidential victory in 1981 was much more favourable than an electoral victory in 1978. First of all, because it was the presidential election, and because it put him in a position, given the logic of the political arrangements he had initially fought against, to benefit from them and to be the true arbiter of those institutions and of politics, to deal the cards. He took full advantage of this.

In any case it so happened that the context had changed and, as you pointed out in the introduction, this electoral victory came at the same time as the electoral victories of Thatcher and Reagan that marked the turning point and the beginning of neoliberal counter-reform in Britain and the United States . As a result, the suspense in France did not last very long. Some people, including ourselves, may have been under a certain illusion with this victory of the left, which explained the euphoria, a little ridiculous in retrospect, that was expressed on the evening of 10 May 1981. It seems like a very long time ago. Since 1958, there had been more than twenty years of the right wing in power. So there was a sense of relief, but beyond the relief, there was the illusion that Mitterrand could finally have a bit of de Gaulle-like ambition.

In terms of ambition, there were the social measures of the first Mauroy government.[145] There was the Cancun speech, which was somewhat in the tone of de Gaulle's speeches in Phnom Penh or the much more timid one in Montreal.[146] But it was a brief episode and, finally, when it had to be decided in 1983, a real turn towards *rigueur* (tight control – spending discipline) was chosen. It was not a policy that could be defined as a social policy. A real step backwards.

It is not very well-known today when we look at the monetary disorder, the financial crisis, etc. – that France, with Fabius as Prime Minister and Beregovoy as Finance Minister, was a pioneer in financial deregulation at the time. It was in the vanguard of what eventually allowed the banks to work closely with state and merchant banks, to embark on financial speculation. This goes hand in hand with the European single market policy of 1986, of course, which was a precursor, and a key link in the construction of a neoliberal Europe.

This is a logical turning-point, if you like, in terms of the political history of Mitterrand as a political personality. It had a real impact.

There was a choice between two policies: a reformist policy, neither subversive nor revolutionary, but one that would have been possible with devaluation, with a battle for the public sector, including elements of protectionism – symbolized by the story of the import of Japanese video recorders.[147] Was a French industrial policy favoured at the time or not? A protectionist policy can be justified if it is accompanied by social measures and social rights. It is explicable and defensible. If it is simply a nationalist policy of 'Making it in France' to which Le Pen added 'French jobs for French workers', that is something else. But that debate took place. It was clearly decided in the direction of a policy that today we would call social-liberal, but that term was not used then.

I remember, I had to analyse the cultural policy of Lang and Mitterrand during this period. Again, it is amazing. If you read Mitterrand's and Lang's speeches before 1981, it is class struggle in culture. The texts are absolutely staggering. In fact, even on that front, we have the impression that the turn to *rigueur* or the so-called turn of 1983 also translates into the Versailles water-jet policy, basically great festivals as a cultural policy, even if the retail price maintenance of books was not dropped.

So, I think the balance sheet, if you look back, is that these Mitterrand years profoundly demoralized and disoriented the left, causing lasting damage to the workers' movement. Moreover, this happened after the twenty or so years of right wing government under de Gaulle, Giscard, etc.

This led, in a way, to the co-option and recycling of a good part of the 1968 generation and of the 1970s, with what we could call a Mitterrand promotion, that is to say a career promotion in the state apparatus and in the administrative apparatus. It recuperated the energies of a large part of those who had been militants, including the leaders of the movements of the 1970s.

So, the balance sheet is that his project lasted, in total, with the interlude of 1986-88, fourteen years, and that Mitterrand won a victory. In other words he had precisely achieved the programme he had set himself in 1968 and radically transformed the landscape of the workers' movement in France, at least on the left, by initiating the death agony of the PCF and the transformation of the Socialist

Party, not only ideologically but socially, into a party for the management of the republican state, a privileged partner for the bosses and an agent for building a neoliberal Europe.

So, beyond the transformation of the political landscape, I believe that the Mitterrand years and especially the 1980s were bleak from the point of view of the social movements and the radical left. The 1990s are already years of rebirth or recovery with the strikes of 1995. In other words, the trade union movement itself, not just the leadership, was collaborating under Mitterrand. The leadership was paralysed in the face of a left government that was pursuing a policy of attacking social gains. That is fairly classic. We saw it again in 1995, when struggles resumed. We saw it again as soon as Jospin came to government: once again, the social movement put itself in the position of a pressure group, of lobbying, but was finally neutralized by the presence of the left in the government.[148]

And from this point of view, the 1980s, taken as a whole, were horrible years. But in addition, I believe, because, beyond the policies, timid at best, or the collaboration of the main trade union leaderships, there was a disorientation that came from the change of period, even at the level of intermediate militants, in the shop stewards or trade-union activists.

That is to say, they were used to managing a social compromise, the one that was negotiated, from a weak position, by the dominant classes at the end of the war, which we can call the social state, Keynesian pact, welfare state, and so on. They managed this in a context of growth, in agreements and conventions. Then they found themselves caught up in a new situation, similar to many other European countries, facing a new aggressivity, especially from the employers and the dominant classes. It is true that in France, 1981-83 marked a turning point. But the whole decade of the 1980s was a decade of defeats, and not only in France, but on a European scale, for the workers' movement. The most emblematic was the defeat in 1984-85 of the British miners, of whom Thatcher wanted to make a real example.

It was less noticed, but in Italy we had the repeal of the sliding scale of wages clauses, for example, which had been a given since the Liberation. In other words, a challenge, unequal according to the balance of power, but methodical, of social gains and I believe a profound disorientation of the organizing cadre more generally, who were no longer fighting in the same context with the same interlocutors and the same rules of the game as in the past thirty years.

These teams had been formed precisely within the last thirty years. This is also true at the political level.

I think you can say what you like about the old bureaucrats of the PCF and the CGT, but the people who had been part of the Popular Front, the war and the Liberation, like Benoît Frachon[149], had a different experience of social struggle, or the leaders of the PCF themselves, than the generation that was born and brought up on the bottle of the Common Programme, which never knew anything else or imagined anything else as a political orientation than electoral victory in alliance with the SP and what is more in a subordinate position.. So all of this, combined, political disorientation, social attacks, and finally real defeats suffered, marks a turning point in the balance of power in the 1980s, which is true in France and at a European level.

14

9 November 1989: The fall of the Berlin Wall

The twentieth century was opened with the 1917 revolution in Russia. Eighty-two years later, on the evening of 9 November 1989, the Berlin Wall fell and hundreds of thousands of East and West Germans immediately crossed the border that had been closed for decades.

But soon in Hungary, Poland and elsewhere, events were developing and the authorities in the so-called communist regimes were vacillating. In the years following the events of 1989, we see collapse of the communist regimes, one after the other. When we remember this period, it is of course because it embodies the end of a world largely polarized in two camps. This raises several questions. Does it, as Eric Hobsbawm has written, bring the twentieth century to a close?[150] And therefore what happened during this short twentieth century in Eastern Europe? Or, to put it another way, what else collapsed apart from the Wall?

The fall of the Berlin Wall is certainly a powerful date and symbol.

Without a doubt we can consider that it marks the end of a series of great events that Hobsbawm, and other historians after him, called the 'short twentieth century'. This short century did not necessarily begin on 1 January 1900, but it began with the war and the Russian Revolution, and it ended with the fall of the Berlin Wall which was followed by the disintegration of what was once the Soviet Union. That, I think, is a pretty obvious observation.

Something has come to an end, but what?

Personally, I am tempted to say that it was a longer cycle which is coming to an end today, which is that of the modern political formations. But that is another discussion.

So what has happened in the twentieth century?

I believe that there was a great defeat for the hopes of emancipation as they existed at the beginning of the twentieth century. I often like to mention an extract from the film by Margarethe Von Trotta about Rosa Luxemburg.[151] There is in it a powerful the image for me. It is a fictional moment in which we see on 1 January 1990 the historical figures of German Social Democracy, Kautsky, Bernstein, Rosa Luxemburg, Bebel, celebrating together the new century as if it was the century that would bring about the end of wars and exploitation, and a peaceful and fulfilled humanity.[152]

Of course one can say that it ended in defeat! But what was that defeat?

One is often tempted to stress the ideological aspect of the defeat. The first attempt to move towards a socialist society failed, and as a result, it jeopardizes new attempts to create something other than a capitalist society, which we can see is heading for a brick wall.

I believe that before considering the ideological or political aspect of the defeat itself, it must be said that it was a social defeat. The disintegration of the Soviet Union, the adoption by the Chinese bureaucracy of a liberal economy, the events in Eastern Europe, the developments in India, all mean that in the last fifteen years there has been a doubling of the labour force available on the world market. Hundreds of millions of workers have suddenly appeared with practically no rights or social protection, until something happens, as it certainly will do. We can see that there are social struggles in China at the moment. There is no reason why Chinese workers should accept the living conditions that European workers refused to accept at the end of the nineteenth century. The problem is that this will take time, and meanwhile the consequence is a deterioration of the balance of social power on a global scale which will have a lasting impact. But this does not mean that we should regret the regimes that existed in the past. We will come back to that

We are at the beginning of a period of reconstruction of trade-union movements, of political forces, including of the redefinition of politics.

Obviously, the moral aspect of the defeat is very important. Confronted with the atrocities of colonization, the horrors of nineteenth century capitalist exploitation described in the novels of Dickens and Zola, the nascent labour and socialist movement had some kind of moral legitimacy. This legitimacy has today been largely lost or at least it has dissolved in the memory that remains of what was bureaucratic or totalitarian despotism.

The word totalitarian, after all, is not embarrassing, as long as, when talking about Stalinist totalitarianism or Nazi totalitarianism, both similarities and differences are stressed. This is something that phony historians like Stéphane Courtois usually forget to do.[153] But this phenomenon does exist, hence the importance today of knowing what happened.

The dominant discourse is to consider that there is some kind of inevitability in the chain of ideas and that there is an inbuilt perversity in the revolutionary or emancipatory project. This means that by wanting to create happiness one creates instead misfortune, dictatorship or even worse.

This is why it is important, beyond ideological discourses, to study the sociology and the history of what happened in the twentieth century, especially in the Soviet Union but also in China.

If we believe that there is a strict continuity between the Russian Revolution of 1917 and the Stalinist regime or its senile successors under Brezhnev, or Andropov, then the conclusion that must be drawn is that the Russian Revolution, as some people said at the time, was not only premature but it was also dangerous and fatal to try to force the course of history.[154] Now that the Soviet archives are open, the serious study of what happened has begun, although much of this work lies ahead of us.

With material that Left Oppositionists did not have in the 1930s, historians like Hobsbawm, and perhaps even more so Moshe Lewin, have been able to show the growth of a huge bureaucratic state apparatus in a country that had a weak structure at the end of the war.[155] The number of state officials grew in just seven years from just over four million in 1927 to more than seventeen million 1934.

That is a dramatic upheaval. No country in the world experienced a rate of urbanization and industrialization like that of the Soviet Union in those years. One tends to see or imagine the Soviet Union of those years as a flabby country like it was in its final years. On the contrary, there was an extraordinary bureaucratic dynamism, the social cost of which was of course exorbitant. It was a modernization by means of whips and floggings, and in which the camps also played an economic function for a kind of primitive accumulation.

But there is no continuity.

Let us be clear, I am certainly not trying to say that the early years of the Russian Revolution of the 1920s were radiant while the 1930s were total darkness. It is more nuanced than that. There were already alarming signs during Lenin's lifetime of bureaucratization, of the professionalization of power, particularly as a consequence of the civil war. We must not forget this.

There is an absolutely terrifying story, *Le Tchékiste*, by Zazubrin.[156] It describes the experience of the political police during the civil war, and we can see very clearly the logic of political violence. The author does not do this to denounce it. He is himself a former Chekist. But he describes as a participant a certain logic of power and violence that is terrifying, even if it is not at that time on the scale of what it became in the 1930s.

Furthermore, political penal colonies began with the opening of the Solovsky Islands colony in 1923. This was before Lenin's death and when the civil war had been won. These were not penal colonies to respond to the situation in the civil war, but political repression after the civil war.

The social and economic turning point after the civil war was missed. The message of the New Economic Policy, which had been debated, was that the war is over and there must be an economic opening.[157] One might logically have thought that this should have also been accompanied by a political opening, by democratization and of course by the end of the state of emergency that could have been considered as necessary during the civil war. But the opposite happened. There was a hardening and a strengthening of the means of repression, a limitation of freedom of speech, and so on. Even if one can detect the seeds of the bureaucratic danger as early as the first years of the Russian Revolution, this does not mean that there is an absolute continuity.

The rupture, which we call a bureaucratic counter-revolution, is not just a word. In the Great Purges of the 1930s, there were millions of deportees and hundreds of thousands of executions between 1933 and 1937. Sloppy historians will sometimes lump together all those who died in the First World War, the Second World War and during the famines. But even if we make a more accurate count of the victims of bureaucratic repression, it still means millions of deaths in the 1930s. And that is of those that we know of. We must also add the Bolshevik Party activists and cadres, 90 per cent of whom disappeared in 1917.

So there is a discontinuity, including in the political personnel. This owes much to a culture of brutality during the civil war that developed in people who were educated in that period, who have been called the *Tsaritsyne* group.

It reminds me of something that we have perhaps already talked about, which was the film about Cambodia, *The Killing Fields*.[158] What has been underestimated is the lasting effect on the minds and in the attitudes of people who suffered the atrocious war in Indochina with nearly twenty or thirty years of bombings. But the war of 1914-18 followed by three or four years of civil war does not justify everything that happened. On the other hand, it does explain it.

I believe that this is a necessary work of clarification. We need to confront the enigma in order to understand what happened to all of us who were at last dreaming of another world.

It is up to all of us to draw not absolute guarantees, but at least some lessons for the future. If we do not do this work, if we stay on the surface of things, then the conclusion is that Rousseau gave birth to Marx, who in turn gave birth to Lenin, who then gave birth to Stalin. It is a genealogy that is found in the first pages of the Bible where everything is linked by filiation. If you believe that, then you should not even try to change the world because it is too dangerous. We must not touch it, we must let it be, and we certainly should not have done this or that.

We are interested in not just observing history or the events that occurred, but in seeing where there were other paths, or other opportunities that were missed or simply lost. We also need to remember that the Bolsheviks themselves were aware of the dangers.

When Lenin danced in the snow because the revolution had lasted a few days longer than the Paris Commune, he was aware of the fragility of the situation. It was already a miracle that it could have lasted so long in a country devastated like Russia. But in the rational idea that he had of society, the Russian revolution only made sense if it was followed up by the revolution in Germany and elsewhere in Europe. This did not occur for reasons discussed elsewhere. Why the German revolution of 1918 to 1923 was defeated is another chapter in history. But once it had been defeated, what can we do? Handing back the power saying to ourselves: 'as it is not going as planned, we are withdrawing and giving you back the keys,'? That is idealistic and not how things happen.

Moshe Lewin, for example, insists on a major issue that we often do not even think about. He says that between February and October in Russia in 1917, the problem was not between insurrection, the Soviet regime and a very respectable parliament such as the British Parliament. The democratic option was not overthrown by the Bolsheviks, it collapsed by itself. The choice was no longer between the February democratic regime and the soviets, but between the military coup and the soviets. So not to fight was to put your head on the chopping block. You do not choose the moment or the time to fight in a struggle with several protagonists.

Nevertheless, the fact remains that the Stalinist counter-revolution was victorious.

This reveals a phenomenon that even the most thoughtful of the Bolsheviks did not see coming and which is not particular to the Soviet Union. It is the role of the bureaucratic phenomenon in contemporary societies, whatever they may be. The complexity of their society, the greater the division of labour, and the development of expertise, all engender a bureaucratization of the state apparatus, political parties, trade-unions and the administration. Bureaucratic temptation is greater in countries that are less culturally developed. Remember how low the literacy rate was in Soviet Russia after the civil war.

This was experienced in Brazil where social inequalities are very high. The slightest privilege takes on proportions that we simply do not have at home. The cultural means to fight bureaucratization are weaker. It is easy to say with hindsight that the Bolsheviks made a big mistake in the early years of the revolution when they only considered the danger of being overthrown by the European counter-revolution. This was not an imaginary danger. European armies had landed in Georgia, led by the French General Weygand amongst others. They only imagined the scenario of being defeated by the European armed reaction, but not of being defeated from within by a bureaucratic gangrene.

This is a lesson that is still being paid for today and from which lessons must be learned. There is no absolute weapon against this bureaucratic danger. But there are the principles of pluralism, of the independence of trade-union and mass organizations, of the relationship of political parties with the organs of power, such as collectives, self-management councils, soviets or other similar structures.

There are major lessons to be learned now that we know the nature of this second danger, that of internal decomposition. Sometimes, being defeated from within is much harder than being defeated by an enemy we know and which is front of us. You can be defeated by an external enemy and not be 'stained', whereas a defeat from the inside is a double defeat. It is a social defeat and it is also a moral defeat. I believe that this is also part of the balance sheet of the century that we will be paying for in the years to come. Even those who opposed and denounced the internal decomposition will be paying for it. When there is a defeat of that size, everyone pays a price, even if unevenly.

A few final words. In 1989, when the Berlin Wall came down, one might have thought that history was finally going to pick up where it left off. I remember a speech by Ernest Mandel[159] at the Mutualité in which he said that what was happening in Germany was a revolution with the masses in the streets of East Germany shouting 'We are the people'. And if we are the people, then who are the others? Who are those in power? If we are the people, they are something else. What is the name of this thing? The Stasi, the bureaucracy, the state apparatus? Mandel said that it was the closing of a parenthesis, and what was happening in East Germany was the renewal of the link with the great period of Rosa Luxemburg and of workers' councils. We were very perplexed because we had been feeling for some time that the break had lasted too long and that the threads of memory had been broken. Indeed, we were aware of what was happening in the Soviet Union, by following the news – there was a Soviet press that we read in the 1980s. There was no longer any possibility to say that in the Soviet Union, with the fall of the regime, it was all going to start again where the debate on the forms of development had been left between Bukharin, Trotsky, and the Left Opposition. Nobody knows Bukharin anymore, nobody knows Trotsky anymore.[160] Maybe they will be rediscovered. But this was no longer at all on the agenda. There are no parentheses in history. There are no detours. Events take place and the consequences are lasting. You could already sense that something was going to change.

What is sad in all this, even for those who fought against this Soviet regime, who have no regrets, who do not consider the fall of the Berlin Wall to be the end of communism because it was no longer communism at all, was that this was the final decomposition of a corpse that had begun to rot forty years previously. In a way, it was a clean-up operation.

The page had to be finally turned to start afresh and to be able to do something else.

But the fact is that, however rotten these regimes were, their fall changed the world balance of forces. These regimes were not models, but they played a small role in the tipping of the balance of forces between the Soviet Union and the United States in Africa or in the Arab world. It is not by chance that in the same year 1989, there was the Ochoa trial in Cuba, which was a bureaucratic hardening of the Cuban regime, and two years later we had the Gulf War.[161] I think what sums up this change in the balance of power is that in Germany, we went very quickly from the rallying cry of 'we are the people' in East Germany during the period of mobilization against Honecker's East German regime, to that of 'we are a people', which is something quite different.[162] It means 'we are the reconstituted Germany' or that Germany has found itself again. Obviously one could only be in favour of German reunification, but without being fooled by the meaning it takes if it is a victory for West German capitalism and a resurrection of German nationalism.

15

For a strategic Marxism

ISABELLE GARO

The publication of this book is very welcome in a period of ongoing struggles when capitalism is in crisis but so are its alternatives. These interviews deal with crucial historical events but above all they open a door to the strategic thinking of Daniel Bensaïd. The essence of his thinking has always had three strong bases: theoretical debates, past struggles and the battles of his time. This was never a rigid or fixed framework, but he lived his life and produced his work within those three dimensions. It this dynamic which is so relevant for us. These interviews are both striking and reflective, committed yet nuanced. They highlight Daniel Bensaïd's specific value among the Marxists of his generation. He was a tireless researcher as well as an activist, someone who drew on the heritage of the workers' movement but was also one of its protagonists and particularly active in the Fourth International.

Whether one agrees or not with all the analyses and political options presented here, the fundamental relevance of such an approach, that we might call both looking backwards and forwards, is without doubt attractive to all those who want to get rid of capitalism before it destroys humanity and nature itself. This is quite different from fashionable counter-factual history but also a long way from resignation and micro-politics. Rather it is about thinking events as a succession of forks in the road, never inevitable nor random, circumstances are changed by the human action that emerges from these contexts but is never limited to that. Essentially it is about approaching politics as a strategic art, combining thought and action, past history and the current situation without confusing them or uncoupling them, nor forgetting that the battle of ideas has always been part and parcel of emancipatory struggles.

There is a worsening crisis of the traditional workers' movement, of both its political and trade-union wings, whilst at the same time rebellion is on the rise worldwide and mobilizations are diversifying and extending. This proves how absolutely urgent it is to renew theoretically informed and politically engaged strategic thinking that is also open, questioning and hopefully collectively discussed. Such a project is immense and goes beyond what is indicated in these interviews with Daniel Bensaïd from ten years ago. He would have probably partly changed them today. For someone who thinks strategically, the past only makes sense in the light that the present casts on it, not as retrospective illusions but as a common perspective and with obvious discontinuities. So through defeats and beyond them we have this dialectic interweaving of ruptures, failures and revolts which cannot be extinguished and provides a particular consistency to the stubborn history of the oppressed.

It remains the case however that in our present chaotic times feelings of failure and fatalism dominate, leading us to only remember the disasters, the mistakes, the diversions and the crimes. Given these conditions a key question is raised: how is Daniel Bensaïd's political Marxism still relevant? He was hostile to politically dogmatic

Marxism and to its academic sterilization, rejecting the division of revolutionary practice between pure theoreticians and registered activists. Daniel Bensaïd was one of the rare Marxists of recent times to keep open the possibility of political Marxism, one which is politically involved and politically interventionist, risking mistakes and dead ends, defeats but also recoveries and upsurges. We should add that such an approach has nothing to do with a self-proclaimed political Marxism where a political line leads and uses Marxism as a post-facto justification. This has been seen many times and it confuses the processes of reflection and of decision-making.

In any case are the current circumstances so unfavourable to Marxism and revolution, to this combination of thinking and intervention of which Daniel Bensaïd was such a tireless partisan? Certainly the communist project is no longer today a collective dream. It is remarkable that for such a resolute anti-Stalinist 1989 was not so much the collapse of bureaucratic 'socialism' as 'a great defeat for the hopes of emancipation' (see p.100 in this book). The perspective of the abolition of capitalism, far from being built as a credible alternative has foundered at the same time as the 'star of October' has dimmed (see p. 12). Instead we see the worsening crisis of capitalism on every level which will end in unthinkable barbarism if nothing is changed urgently. The current situation is dramatically blocked as a result of decades of capitalism's devastating neo-liberal policies bringing increasing inequality, exploitation, precarious work, political and military repression of protests, attacks on migrants, ravaging of the environment and rival imperialisms at each others' throats.

We have not been able to, or known how to, break out of the steel cage of capitalism. But history does not end even on this failure, the causes of which we need to understand. Thinking through the possible outcomes of yesterday, quite different but still inseparable from the possible outcomes of today, is to break the false linearity of a history that is always retrospectively conceived as inevitable. This is not the approach taken by Daniel Bensaïd who points out in one of the interviews: 'We are interested in not just observing history or the events that occurred, but in seeing where there were other paths, or other opportunities that were missed or simply lost,' (p. 104-5).

In this sense, a picture of the contemporary situation painted from the sole angle of the long defeat of the workers' movement leads one to judge any emancipatory struggle to be over before it starts, or to be definitively doomed to failure. Such a picture lacks the essential element: the central role of contradictions, both objective and subjective (which are usually over-differentiated). Contradictions condition the disintegration of politics, the untimely setback of criticism and the perpetual resurgence of conflict in class societies, which is its very motor while being largely concealed.

Thus, Daniel Bensaïd would certainly have been attentive to the resurgence of mobilizations throughout the world, the new feminist wave, the rise of climate mobilizations, democratic demands, the struggles of working-class neighbourhoods against police violence, established racism and Islamophobia, struggles that are closely intertwined with traditional workplace protests. Perhaps he would have modified some analyses of the past in their light, since he refused to dissociate past history from the reasons we still have for being interested in it.

These contradictions are essential and are constitutive of all class societies, sharpened in times of widespread and generalized economic, social and political crisis, as is the case today. The specific task of political Marxism is to propose an analysis – always to be readjusted – of the way these contradictions cross, structure and destabilize capitalist social relations. But they also run through the individuals themselves, all the exploited and dominated of the world, dividing them between acquired capacities and alienation, between stolen time and the will to really live, between forced consent, deviated hope and relentless resistance: this dialectic is not a philosophical view, it is embodied in the very flesh of things and provides the possibility of their transformation.

The first condition for this possibility is the active and conscious politicization of these contradictions, the construction and rebuilding of social and political forces educated about the past and carrying an alternative for today. For this is or should be the hallmark of living Marxism, when it cultivates dialectical attention to reality: knowing how to detect in defeat not the conditions for the ineluctable victory of tomorrow, but the renewed exploration of the possible. The latter exists at the heart of the fundamental instability of a capitalism that, more than ever, needs threats and terror to reproduce and maintain itself.

Thus, humanity, sitting on an unprecedented powder keg, is facing a new episode in the long-term economic crisis of contemporary capitalism. It is even more serious than the previous one, but it never leads, by itself, to an emancipatory upsurge. It can just as easily end up in the worst regression and fascism. Contemporary catastrophism paralyses just as much as the once immoderate confidence of a Kautsky or faith in the infinite resilience of capitalism. In any case, what is missing is the transformative will, the critical awareness of the stakes involved and of the concrete circumstances, as well as a political structuring of class struggles. Only class struggle is capable of reorienting the course of history and of engaging the long and difficult task of the democratic and co-ordinated abolition of capitalism.

The analysis of historical crossroads is central to Daniel Bensaïd's thinking. How relevant this is to the unprecedented juncture that our present has become. We face many dangers but few alternatives and time is running out. And if Marxism remains indispensable to think and transform our potentially nightmarish historical trajectory, it is because this political contradiction, if we extend the analysis, leads right to the heart of the social relations of capitalism. To that nodal point of the relations of exploitation where wage earners, selling their labour power, makes capitalist accumulation possible while trying to resist the theft of their time and lives.

While this resistance is only a potential outcome, it is from this ever-vibrant basis that we can see emerge the rejection of a mode of production based on class domination and the exploitation of labour, on the crushing of all the capacities, of the very being of men and women. 'Individuals have always built on themselves,' Marx affirmed.[163] The corollary of this affirmation is the obstinate construction of resurgent and combative forms of solidarity, carrying within them the seeds of a completely different political and social organization.

In this respect, Daniel Bensaïd is decidedly one of the rare great Marxists of our time, for not having abandoned the idea of a critique of political economy as a theoretical and militant priority. He understood the possibility of a global understanding, which does not crush specificity, which does not submit to any pre-written scenario or to any over-riding authority, but which does not abandon the idea of a worldwide emancipation achieved along different roads.

Untiringly dismantling preconceived ideas about Marx and Marxism, polemicizing head to head with all the reigning ideologies, Daniel Bensaïd has been able to maintain and keep alive the articulation of (never finished) theoretical work and of militant intervention, which is just as ongoing, difficult and uncertain. For the relevance of political Marxism, given its inescapably critical and militant dimensions, is above all a task. I want to conclude by making three points.

The first is that despite a social and political relationship of forces that is not very favourable to workers and the oppressed in general, radical political dissent has not disappeared. It is clearly taking on new forms and developing a project which is appropriate for our historical times. The renewed interest in Marx and Marxism, however much it represents a minority of the movement, is both a cause and consequence of these struggles.

The second remark concerns the history of socialism and of the political movements which have more or less claimed to be Marxist and are considered in these interviews focussed on a series of key dates from 1917 to 2007. In order not to become disorientated we need to know this history, to discuss it, to take part in the great political debates of the workers' movement.

The third remark is that political Marxism, conceived in this way, can only live today on the twofold condition of always being reinvented and readjusted to the circumstances of our time, that is to say to its contradictions and to the space for intervention that they open up. This adjustment is not – cannot be – the result of pure thought: it is the product of collective political work, located at the meeting point of analysis and practical, social and political experiences at a given time. The revival of this work is of the utmost importance today.

Therefore, in line with these considerations, one can outline a basic strategic agenda, taking note of the main dilemmas that today paralyse the political reconstruction of the alternative: short-sighted pragmatism or maintaining an ultimate but inaccessible horizon as well as an illusory 'already there'; bypassing the state or institutional integration; dispersal of struggles or unity decreed from above. The question of refashioning a mobilizing perspective, the invention of a desirable and possible common future, but also of new forms of organization rooted in existing structures and political culture, is a collective, urgent task.

How can a unitary project be re-founded on the basis of social and political protests as they exist and are being transformed today? The classic axes of the socialist and communist alternative: the state and the party, property and work, must be reinvested, but taking into account the fact that they are now crossed and recomposed by the equally decisive questions of ecology and antifascism, race and gender. These struggles are not sides, but the very forms of contemporary class struggle that challenge traditional strategies. The most urgent political task is undoubtedly to abandon all subordination to one another, but not only to disperse them.

One of the key words of Daniel Bensaïd's work and of the Marxism he defends, is democracy. We can achieve democracy if genuinely democratic organizations are maintained and expanded, anticipating in the present the true democracy to come, going beyond but not rejecting the crisis-ridden parliamentary forms. It is only if there is a collective intellectual elaboration that a Marxism of today can exist and bring about, or at least sketch out, the social and political commons that alone can put an end to the reign of the capitalist law of value. The specificity of strategic reflection is clear here: it has to do with the autonomy of politics, detaching it from an approach that focuses only on the objective historical context. .

This book of interviews shows Daniel Bensaïd's extreme attention to concrete circumstances and their dialectic, his qualities of incessant questioning, acute intelligence, immense culture, open-mindedness and unremitting militancy. All these qualities are required by the revolution of our times, in the midst of the maze of the present, of the ongoing attacks but also of revolts and anger. For it is now quite clear that only our educated, questioning and organized anger will be successful.

16

Saving politics?

OLIVIER NEVEUX

Daniel Bensaïd did not write much, if anything at all, directly on what is now generally called 'neoliberalism'. He died a few months after the debates eventually unfolded on its characterization. In fact, it is from 2009 onwards in France, with the publication of *La Nouvelle raison du monde* by Pierre Dardot and Christian Laval (Ed. La Découverte, 2010) that neoliberalism ceases to be the scarecrow it was until then among many activists. Part of the debate is around the term neoliberalism or, rather, 'anti-neoliberalism', which is suspected of dissolving the anticapitalist sharpness of the struggle or, on the contrary, credited with favouring a unitary dynamic. Bensaïd joins in the debate:

> We are anti-capitalists because we fight social injustice, because we are ecologists, feminists, anti-militarists. That word is not sufficient to define a project, but it has the merit of clearly designating the enemy. Anti-neoliberalism can constitute a common minimum basis for global justice movements,

calling for the cancellation of third world debt, against tax havens, etc. But it is a broad concept, bringing together both Brazilian President Lula da Silva and Evo Morales in Bolivia, class struggle trade unionists and the bureaucrats of the European Trade Union Confederation, as well as opponents and supporters of the European Union liberal treaties. Anti-liberalism can facilitate the struggle and joint action, but it is not a solid basis for building a party that not only wants to change society but wants to have a different type of society.[164]

The identification, not without contradictions, from 2010 onwards of 'neoliberalism' shifted the focus. The term makes it possible to characterize the various contemporary forms that capitalism is taking, but also the ideology that naturalizes it, the 'shock strategy' which it applies, the theoretical yeast that made it rise such as those of the Walter Lippmann colloquium or of the Mont-Pelerin Society.[165] 'Neoliberalism', in its diversity, is therefore understood as a sequence of capitalism, with its elements and components, its novelties and continuities, or rather as 'a period of late capitalism'.[166] Bensaïd speaks little about this, if at all.

Nevertheless, he does not leave us totally helpless in the face of the neoliberal offensive, whose onset he situates 'at the turn of the 1980s, under Thatcher and Reagan'.[167] This is not very surprising: he is constantly on the lookout in his writings for the transformations at work in each situation, always being attentive to the dialectic that weakens that which is stable and undermines that which is established. In fact, the many texts he published in the 2000s take into account what was then changing: 'The question therefore is not that of the disappearance of classes, but that of the metamorphosis of the wage-earners, of the uncertainties about their future, of the struggles in which their new representations are elaborated.'[168] Bensaïd picks out the class war that is now taking place, noting however that: 'The class war is in reality only one of the facets of a global state of war declared immediately after the attacks of 11 September 2001', and he then reflects on the state of emergency, even if it means reopening, legitimately, the works of the Nazi philosopher Carl Schmitt.[169]

Despite being attentive to changes and mediations, his vision is not an enlightenment, or visionary of the promise of a brighter tomorrow. Not everything that moves is necessarily red. But everything that moves could become red. The approach is to spot the signs that confirm that the situation is not quite what it appears to be, that there are clues that open up its understanding to obvious or tiny possibilities, without exaggerating what its essence or its tendencies. The decisive point is that the analysis of social and political changes must never be disconnected from the analysis of their consequences. 'Neoliberalism' also exists by what it produces in the field of struggles, responses, and the loss of militant traditions. More recent works have stressed the fact that the 'great reactionary wave that was prepared in the 1970s was not so much conceived as an alternative to the welfare state but as an alternative to challenging it. It was an alternative to the alternative.'[170] Proof, if proof was needed, that the analysis of domination without the resistance to it often lacks the decisive elements for its political appreciation. This means paying attention to the 'new social movements', to organizations, to the effectiveness of the class struggle, to the political field, to electoral timetables, to the changes in social democracy and to the left 'rallied to stock market euphoria.'[171] And this is undertaken with 'the obsession with the struggle for power. This is not in a narrow and political sense, nor in the psychological sense of a craving for power, but because it is the key to social emancipation.'[172]

The dynamic of this thinking has become rare enough to be worth noting: in contrast to the numerous studies of neoliberalism, this particular kind of critical work, which brings together valuable, overarching (and divergent) conceptualizations of the implementation of neoliberalism – what it does to 'souls', to lives, to skills, to countries, to the state, to classes – or which makes history by its ideas, Bensaïd's view is inevitably located from the point of view of the struggles *to wage*. The project is military: to intervene. Thought is thus organized corresponding to the tasks of the hour, pitted against the passage of time by the foreboding of the catastrophe to come.[173] Such an approach is full of stakes and assets. Contrary to academic Marxism or theoretical radicalism, the approach does not favour scholarship, a closed system, or a mechanical doctrine, but on the contrary focuses on the breaches, echoes, contradictions, and breakdowns of the moment that are caught between 'no longer and not yet'. It contains the possibilities, sometimes tiny and that are envisaged as such; it opens up hypotheses for action.

And this is how his last great book, *Éloge de la politique profane* begins: on the need for the development of 'a new political vocabulary':

> Capital has its own vocabulary, that of the ventriloquist commodity and its spontaneous vocabulary. Employment is interchangeable with shareholding, exploitation with the spirit of enterprise, work with leisure, collective solidarity with personalized journey. This postmodern jargon of euphemisms and circumlocutions is manufactured and spread out daily: employability and just-in-time, internet-economics, e-business and hedge funds, burn-out and workfare, 'stress management' (!) and 'constrained involvement' (!), lean production and over-worked working poor, governance and administrative management, 'households with random incomes'.[174]

This vocabulary is well known. It is that of neoliberalism, of entrepreneurial glory. Bensaïd does not stop there. The book does not overemphasize the contemporary lament: the recording of our defeats, concessions and retreats. Nor does it predict the imminence of progressive salvation. There is here a methodology:

> A new vocabulary is not artificially invented like a type of Esperanto. It does not arise out of some innocent design. It is born from the conflictual exchange between real languages, from fundamental social and historical experiences, from the struggles of words [...] the discourse of resistance can only escape the vicious circle of subalternity by going to the root of things and going beyond appearances, to extract from experiences that are reflected upon some shards of truth.[175]

It is a very difficult task to inhabit contradiction, to deal with 'the difficult question of the times' and their conflict, to articulate the modesty of what is possible with the immensity of what is necessary, to link the humility of militant acts with the enormity of historical junctions. It means not telling each other stories, understanding what domination does to lives, especially to those who resist and organize, and to associate with the necessary defence, as far as possible, an agenda and a vocabulary that do not allow themselves to be subordinated. The work is theoretical, political and militant. It refers to the battle of ideas that is being played out – without reducing the situation to the latter (there is a tension 'between the theory of neoliberalism and the actual pragmatics of neoliberalization'[176]).

In the framework of Bensaïd's thinking, 'postmodernism' embodies in many ways the ideological shadow of what would later be called 'neoliberalism'. Its role is to be that of a dominant 'thought', with relatively loose contours and yet recognizable as common, and more or less internalized slogans. Postmodernism is the name that Bensaïd uses to characterize the form of the dominant ideology that tends to modify subjectivities, or to justify their modifications, as well as to break the strategic intention: postmodernism is the enterprise of delegitimizing politics, of blurring its conflicting coordinates. In many ways it intersects with what will become the 'neoliberal discourse'. However, it is to be understood not by the ideal purity of ideas but by the standard of the fate of capital, in a tight dialectic which commands in its turn the need for 'an asymmetrical strategy'.[177]

He thus identifies what is happening at the level of what actually exists – what the soon-to-be 'new world' of 'start-up nations' is producing, even as what exists – public services, states, institutions, democracy – is supposed to adopt entrepreneurial logic:

> All this is obviously not without effect on the nature of social relations in contemporary societies. The damage caused by neoliberal policies is considerable. The competition of everybody against each other, the pitting of the exploited against those who are even more exploited, the destruction of old solidarities, all testify to the degree to which neoliberalism has penetrated society.[178]

The observation is remarkable, it refers to what is happening: 'the ideal of a society based on solidarity is replaced by that of a society of generalized competition'.[179] The viewpoint captures both the individual and the world which has in part created it, along with society and national specificities. The critical adventure of political economy includes concern for the totality. The individual dimension, the one that witnesses crushed, standardized and isolated lives, cannot by itself bear witness to what is at stake. It allows, as we know, the most massive and desperate reactionary lamentations about the good old days. Neoliberalism cannot also be analysed by the ultimate yardstick of theory, an idea floating in the air, without ties or institutions, without foundations or movement. Neither can 'neoliberal ideology' and its 'great fantasy', that is the 'complete colonization of social life', be understood as a 'description of what is, but rather as a tool for a total domination of what has not yet happened.'[180] And much, if not everything, is at stake in this 'not yet happened'.

It is necessary to resume: Bensaïd spots the new offensive of capital. It attacks, it is predatory and it transforms itself into a new brutal phase of dispossession and privatization. Certainly he sees it now more in the continuity of what it precedes, noting its intensity and its redoubled voracity, rather than its novelty. The change is not substantial. Here, Bensaïd is relatively orthodox: 'The financialization of the economy is an inevitable development of industrial capitalism.'[181] This can be understood. It is a question of not getting rid of words. Capitalism, despite its tricks and ruses, is still capitalism. And it is in Marx that Bensaïd mainly seeks theoretical categories, in order to think about it, to extend its study, wishing to accentuate the contradictions:

> Capitalist profitability has as its criterion the law of value. [...] Now, what sort of work is necessary for writing a computer program by a research establishment? A highly cooperative and socialized work. The more cooperative the work is, the more it incorporates accumulated knowledge, and the more difficult it is to quantify and to measure in terms of abstract work. This seems to me to be one of the key factors of the current social crisis, which means that productivity gains

are not converted into free time but, on the contrary, into social exclusion.[182]

The answer to this (among others) was the launching in 2009 of a New Anticapitalist Party in which Bensaïd played a major role. It is then a good thing to put capitalism back at the centre of what matters. Being anticapitalist is the minimum for want of a broad programmatic perspective and a strong development of strategy. However there is also 'New' and 'Party'. The defence of the party, as we know, is one of the constant themes of Bensaïd's 'libertarian Leninism': the need for organization, which is lost if not taken up. There is in him the constant concern not to rely on the tossing of inconsistent opinions no more than on the truths of a few enlightened sciences:

> The denigration of the party as a form of organization is part of the degradation through plebiscites of political life, of its increasing personalization, of its evolution towards a relationship that merges the charismatic individual with a high media profile and the inorganic mass, in defiance of any political, partisan or other mediation. Now, politics is precisely an art of mediation.[183]

The 'New' is more complex to define. It remains unclear. Is it a change of period? There is a crisis, certainly, because it is against the backdrop of the 2007 crisis that Bensaïd's final reflections are taking shape. But it comes from far away, and even deeper, because:

> This crisis, dragging on indefinitely, is not an ordinary stop-go crisis, with its ups and downs, and the consolation of

telling oneself that things will necessarily get better tomorrow.[...] It is a crisis of civilization. A generalized breakdown of measures and relations, of which the social crisis and the ecological crisis are the two most flagrant manifestations. It is a to short step from this to privatizing the sun and patenting the alphabet and mathematics.[184]

So what can be done? 'The question is on what basis new solidarities can be built today. In my opinion, one of the main tasks facing the radical left is to make class solidarities appear where they are not necessarily perceived.'[185] The proposal is a classic one. To return to class customs, not to allow oneself to be divided, to encourage, construct and consolidate solidarities. There are no solutions in Bensaïd's writings. One can find either that it is insufficient or that it is joyful. He does not have an answer for everything. His thinking is not indifferent to circumstances, nor is it solitary or visionary.

Nevertheless, he has constantly insisted that the answer will not be exclusively social. It will be political, despite the 'crisis of the concept of politics':[186]

> a politics uprooted from all historical determinations and conditions, which would henceforth be reduced to a juxtaposition of day-to-day actions, of floating sequences, without logical links or continuity. The consequence of this narrowing of political temporality around a fleeting present that is always starting over again is to close down all strategic thinking, in the same way that the philosophies of history do.[187]

This would be, perhaps, the primordial challenge: to save politics from what seeks to destroy it:

The privatization of the world leads to a withering of public space and to democratic anaemia. This is illustrated by the fashionable term 'governance': politics reduced to management, expertise and power techniques.[188]

It is important to work on what is urgent (for example, 'reclaiming and transforming public service'[189]) under the stress that politics implies. Hannah Arendt's concern, so often quoted by Bensaïd, about a possible disappearance, one day, of politics feeds his work and his writing. Saving politics from threats, impediments and parodies. This is one of the most terrifying activities of neoliberalism: smothering politics in bureaucracy, replacing it with technocracy, neutralizing it, draining it into consensus, policing and repressing it. This danger presupposes an increased and obsessive attention to what can disseminate democratic experiences, sharpen debates, promote self-organization to win, here and now with balance of forces, but also to what can determine the discussion, development, construction and partial experimentation of this 'other world', which is probably possible and certainly urgent.

17

Ecocommunism or ecology versus capital

CHRISTINE POUPIN

Throughout these *Radio Fragments*, the word ecology has not been uttered once, neither in the questions put to Daniel Bensaïd nor in his answers.

This absence does not do justice to all the pages he has written of theoretical reflection, as well as those enriching the debate with the different currents of political ecology. Moreover Ecocommunism is a term he invented.

The interviews examine the twentieth century, a century which at its heart saw a major shift of geological magnitude. Indeed, the 1950s marked the beginning of what scientists call the Anthropocene.

The term appeared at the dawn of the 21st century when Paul Crutzen, vice-president of the International Geosphere-Biosphere Programme (IGBP), stated that human activity had given birth to a new geological epoch. In 2007, along with other climate scientists Will Steffen and John McNeill, Paul Crutzen clarified the definition of the Anthropocene:

...the Earth has now emerged from its natural geological epoch, the present interglacial period called the Holocene. Human activities have become so pervasive and profound that they rival the great forces of Nature and are pushing the Earth into a planetary *terra incognita*. The Earth is rapidly moving into a less biologically diverse, less forested, much warmer, and probably wetter and stormier state.[190]

This is the work of scientists, not activists or Marxists, but it is of the utmost importance for activists, and not only for ecologists. That is because it allows us, or more precisely, forces us to take stock of the destruction underway, which any emancipatory project must aim at first of all stopping and then repairing.

For nearly 12,000 years, the relatively stable climate of the Holocene epoch has conditioned the evolution of human societies. Moving into another epoch and leaving this relative stability, is to radically alter our conditions of existence. After long and numerous debates, sometimes fraught with ideological bias, to place the beginning of the Anthropocene, a certain degree of scientific consensus now exists to recognize the years following the end of the Second World War as the moment of this geological and social turning point. The numerous impacts on the planet, which exist since the industrial revolution, have now become global and synchronized, whether it be the increase in carbon dioxide and other greenhouse gas emissions, the rendering of land artificial, the decline in biodiversity, the disruption of the cycles of carbon, nitrogen, phosphorus or water, etc. The various data which record these phenomena all show a clear shift at this moment. In the words of John Bellamy Foster: 'the post-war period was characterized by a qualitative transformation in human capacity for destruction.'

Some people prefer the term Capitalocene to Anthropocene, as they believe the latter calls into question human activity in general and masks the responsibility of capitalism. There is a real risk of an essentialist and depoliticized explanation. However, the dating is beyond doubt as it designates a new phase of capitalism involving a quantitative and qualitative transformation of the conditions of production. In the countries of the global North, there was the emergence of industrial agriculture, and of the petrochemical, nuclear power and car industries which opened up an unprecedented increase in mass consumption and a productivist race, in which the USSR and the GDR also participated. For the global South, the consequences were dramatic, especially those of the misnamed 'green revolution'. Colonialism was coupled with environmental racism.

In the interview on 8 May 1945, Daniel underlines the specificity of the moment and of 'the social compromise [...] that made economic growth possible via recovery,' 'a compromise that to some extent made it possible to limit social conflict for three decades, until the end of the 1960s, beginning of the 1970s.' The price paid for this compromise was the dispossession and domination of colonized peoples as well as the destruction and plundering of nature. When he adds that this compromise gave the 'illusion that capitalism had the means of mastering its contradictions and managing them rationally', the dramatic destruction caused by extractivism and productivism shows how deep the illusion was.

This change took place three-quarters of a century ago, and since then the rate at which these events are taking place has accelerated further.

The exhaustion of the post-war phase of growth did not slow down the disaster, on the contrary. The neoliberal antisocial offensive launched in the 1980s was accompanied by a new acceleration of ecological destruction: increased dispossession of water, land and seed resources, an explosion in the transport of goods due to the relocation of production, programmed obsolescence, encouragement of consumption by means of credit, luxury consumption for the richest. The consequences are even greater for the peoples of the South who are the first victims of extractivist policies and of climate change, the destruction of subsistence farming and the dumping of toxic waste.

With the depth of the 2007-2008 crisis, capitalism is looking for new means of accumulation. The so-called green economy aims to revive capitalist growth by dressing itself in the protection of the climate, biodiversity, the oceans, etc. But the remedies of green capitalism are even worse than the evil they claim to fight, they are called: nuclear power, bio-fuels, and clean coal. Under the guise of 'carbon neutral' or 'net zero emissions' strategy, capitalism claims to have found a miracle cure to absorb the CO_2 they refuse to stop emitting because they refuse to move away from fossil fuels. It promotes technologies that are as dangerous as they are inefficient, such as bio-energy with carbon capture and storage (BECCS). BECCS is based on the real capacity of plants to absorb CO_2 during their growth, but gambles in a very risky way on the possibility of capturing and storing the CO_2 emitted during their combustion in a sustainable and reliable way. Above all, BECCS would involve expropriating farmers to divert huge areas of arable land from food production, using chemical fertilisers, pesticides and herbicides on a massive scale, exhausting land and water.

This combination of ecological, social and democratic crises can only encourage us to join John Bellamy Foster's invitation to 'base ourselves on the ecological foundations of Marxist thought in order to tackle capitalism as it is today and the global ecological crisis it has created – as well as the dominant forms of ideology that oppose the establishment of a real alternative'.

An invitation to which Daniel responded at length.

He made a major contribution to the thinking of our current and its understanding of the ecological dimension. This was the case with his paper on 'Marx, productivism and ecology' presented to the conference on ecology held in October 1993 at the International Institute for Research and Education in Amsterdam.

He rejects as 'anachronistic the removal of Marx from the technological optimism and Promethean illusions of his time'. But he also considered it 'abusive to make him a carefree champion of overindustrialization and uninterrupted progress'. He proposes to 'place us in his contradictions' without confusing 'the questions he left open and the answers provided later by the positivist orthodoxy of the social-democratic or Stalinist imitators'. He thus insists on the rupture constituted by the bureaucratic counter-revolution in the Soviet Union, which, in its desire to 'catch up with and overtake the "performance" of capitalism', silenced the pioneers of ecology whose names have been forgotten (Vernadsky, Gause, Kasharov or Stanshinsky) and which was expressed in various publications and congresses (Fourth Pan-Russian Congress of Zoologists in 1930, International Congress of History of Science and Technology in 1930). He points out the incompatibility between on one hand a critical ecology, and on the other the frenzied productivist collectivization and forced industrialization; between the need to consider the global environment, and 'socialism in one country'; between the understanding of the interdependence between human beings and nature, and bureaucratic voluntarism; between the broadest possible democracy applied to production choices, and bureaucratic dictatorship. He invites us to 'walk backwards through these layers of ideological sediments to renew the theoretical dialogue'.

Daniel Bensaïd returns to the 'fertile intuitions' of researchers such as Podolinski, who developed a critique of classical economics from the point of view of taking stock of material or energy resources, or Clausius, who wrote in 1885 on the subject of coal: 'We consume these reserves from now on and we behave like prodigal heirs' but notes that 'unfortunately, the spread of Marxism in parallel with the rise of the mass workers movement is based on a mostly positivist and scientific interpretation'.

Clausius shows to what extent political ecology can nevertheless be a 'formidable counter-myth' in the face of 'capital (which) lives from day to day, in the immediacy of enjoyment and selfishness with no tomorrow'.

In contrast to market reductionism, which would have us believe that real flows and monetary flows obey the same logic because they are exchanged one against the other, Clausius puts back in its squalid place the market – 'which does not satisfy needs but demand'; money – which 'is not the real but its fanciful representation'; and the sphere of the market economy – which 'is never more than a small bubble whose partial rationality works to the detriment of the whole'. He stresses the need to 'reintegrate the economy into a totality of ecological and social determinations'.

He also comes back to the 'productive forces from the point of view of capitalism' which 'can perfectly well prove to be destructive for the future of humanity'. This opens the way to a critique of the very concept of progress.

In an article for *Contretemps* in 2002 entitled 'L'écologie n'est pas soluble dans la merchandise' (Ecology cannot be transformed into a commodity), Daniel Bensaïd conducts a debate with the different currents of political ecology, not without having praised the merit of a critical ecology that 'contributes to undoing the belief in a redemptive end of history where humanity, reconciled with itself, would savour forever and completely time which has been recovered'.

For him, 'ecology has its reasons, which the folly of capital ignores. The care of the ecology of the planet cannot therefore be entrusted to the mechanisms of market regulation'. And he gives the fundamental reason for this:

> There is no common measure between the logic of the market, for which working time is the standard of all things, and the social relation of the natural conditions of reproduction in time and space. [...] This incorrect assessment of the world and its 'squalid' base carries within it the generalized deregulation of social relations as well as the relations between society and the natural conditions of its reproduction.

Daniel Bensaïd polemicizes usefully with different currents: 'a deep fundamentalist ecology, ready to sacrifice humanity to a naturalistic theology; a dogmatic and despotic ecology, based on contested scientific certainties; a reformist and political ecology, devoted to institutional lobbying' and pleads for a 'subversive, popular and militant ecology, feeding all social, trade union and cooperative movements' and this remains a burning issue today.

However, today's reading of this 2002 text reveals the extent to which the reality, but also the perception of this reality, has profoundly changed: the various ecological crises have deepened and accelerated, and they are exacerbating each other. The collapse of the biodiversity is such that we can speak of a sixth extinction of the species. The change in land use (deforestation, extension of cultivated land, drying up of wetlands, etc.) has, for its part, exceeded the critical threshold of danger and is no longer capable of allowing humanity to exist in decent conditions. Climate change represents the most global and immediate danger. Extreme climatic events such as heat waves, droughts, hurricanes or floods are increasing in number and severity, hitting particularly hard the poor and the peoples of the South. In an infernal spiral, the effects of global warming, – gigantic fires, the Amazon forest becoming arid, the melting of permafrost and ice caps, etc. – are each in turn the cause of new increases in temperature, resulting in a rise in sea levels of up to several metres. The drastic reduction of greenhouse gas emissions cannot wait any longer. It requires a massive reduction of the use of fossil fuels, which currently account for the bulk of energy consumption. It is possible and essential to switch to renewable energy sources, but this must be accompanied by an overall reduction in energy consumption and therefore also of production of material goods and their transport.

This makes all the more topical the impossibility, posited by Daniel Bensaïd in 2002, of 'resorting to the convenient joker of abundance, which would make it possible to avoid having to arbitrate and choose on the pretext that everything, no doubt tomorrow or the day after tomorrow at the latest, would become possible and compatible'.

The bulk of destructive production such as the arms industry or a large part of the chemical industry, the over-consumption of luxury goods by the richest, the needs artificially created by advertising, inbuilt obsolescence, the transport of goods to enable multinationals to put their employees in competition with each other, are all proof that it is possible to produce less and transport less while living better and sharing more, as long as we do not overlook issues of ownership and democracy. And to return to Bensaïd's 1993 text, 'Le tourment de la matière':

> An economy that meets popular needs cannot be reduced to monetary or energy calculations. It must strive to hold

both ends at once, in the only way that is possible. Not by quantitative measurement and technocratic expertise, but by informed democratic choice. For when one abandons the illusion of an total socialization of nature just as much as an total naturalization of human beings, then the contradiction is real. There is no point in denying it. One must settle and work within it.

18

Taking leaps seriously

UGO PALHETA

'The twilight of capitalism need not initiate the night of humanity, which, to be sure, seems to threaten today'

Max Horkheimer, *Twilight*, p. 11.

Daniel Bensaïd liked to say that Marxism is 'an inheritance without owners or instruction manuals.' Such a legacy has therefore given rise to countless appropriations, to the extent that in order to emphasize the point, we can talk about its immense variety with 'a thousand Marxisms'. We could legitimately add that Daniel Bensaïd's Marxism lends itself less than any other to a retrospective reconstruction into a dogma (an instruction manual), which could be acquired by a clergy of authorized interpreters (its owners) working to consolidate a unit of followers.

His fierce resistance to thinking in a dogmatic and rigid manner finds its principle in his rejection of all comforting teleology but also of all economism. He was fond of the formula by Marx and Engels in *The Holy Family* according to which 'history is nothing'. This was not simply because it allowed him to reject the tendency to reduce Marx to the rank of a mere philosopher of history, predicting the end of history and universal progress. It was also because it allowed him to insist that history has no end, meaning both that it has no goal and limit, and that it has no conclusion and destination. If men and women live, think and act in conditions that they have not chosen, their future derives in the first instance not from economic trends that are ruthlessly imposed (as can be read in vulgar economism that sometimes masquerades as Marxism), but from the struggles that they lead (or on the contrary refuse, or are unable to lead), the victories that are won or the defeats that are suffered.

Along with Daniel Bensaïd, we have to get rid once and for all of history with a capital H, in order to replace it with a history that is profane, necessarily chaotic, and conceived as a dynamic of social relations that unavoidably generates conflicts whose outcomes are unpredictable. If history has no direction or destiny without guarantee, then 'one can only predict "scientifically" the struggle' as Gramsci put it. Hence those 'leaps' which Daniel Bensaïd made the title of one of his most penetrating articles.[191] Borrowing the formula from Lenin in his *Philosophical Notebooks*, whose theoretical and strategic figure Daniel Bensaïd did much to restore, the 'leaps' allow him to identify moments of historical rupture, of crossroads, in other words of breaches that can suddenly open up and then close again no less suddenly if the opportunity is not grasped or if the initiative is not taken by the subalterns.

This attention to the non-linear time of non-professional and desanctified politics, or what he called at the end of his life the politics of the oppressed, is reflected in every interview in this book. Daniel Bensaïd always insisted on reintegrating the event he was examining into a long view of history, on measuring its effects that are often far from being without ambiguity, and on strenuously opposing all one-way interpretations of history, whether reactionary or 'progressive'. For him, it is a question of taking seriously the 'leaps', the moments of social confrontation and political struggle. It is in those moments when the state of things, which is also the state of bodies and minds, is fragmenting, when long-held popular aspirations can finally be proudly expressed (think of May-June 1968!), when the economic struggle is shifting to the political field, that millions of people will discover possibilities which were not obvious, often just the day before.

Apart from these very particular situations of popular uprisings, which sometimes manage to become authentic revolutions, the ruling classes manage to restrict and narrow down effectively the field of possibilities. Before the vast strike movement and the occupation of factories in 1936, very few thought it was possible to be paid without having to work. The mobilization nevertheless made it possible to win paid holidays, which according to the employers and the right, would have put the whole of French industry out of business! This was obviously not the case. And even when the oppressed are defeated, there is always something left of their movement: the wealthy fear that their privileges can be taken away, which in itself is important to wrest concessions from them in the future, and the dispossessed still hope to see their oppression end. The event therefore does two things: it actually enables us to conquer, but it also allows us to glimpse at the 'lateral possibilities' (to use Pierre Bourdieu's beautiful expression). There are many possibilities whose conditions of realization – a sufficiently massive, united and radical mobilization – cannot not (temporarily) be met, but which point towards a future of emancipation.

I would now like to come back to the question of the legacy or, more precisely, of the ways in which to inherit Marxism from Daniel Bensaïd. This is based on my work on the conditions for the re-emergence of a fascist danger in contemporary capitalist societies, particularly in France.[192] I will do this by making the link with certain fundamental elements of his thought, and I will try to show how they allow us to grasp the features of our present political situation in relation to the question of fascism (of which we will not find any specific elements of analysis in his work).

Marxism can rightly be seen as a way of thinking about a crisis, but this is particularly true of Daniel Bensaid's Marxism, and furthermore this makes his work a fundamental tool for us today. From the end of the 1980s onwards, the author of *Marx l'intempestif* [193] was clearly a descendant of Walter Benjamin (to whom he devoted an important work[194]), distancing himself from an ideology of progress long associated with a certain kind of Marxism: that of the Second International represented by Karl Kautsky, considered at the time as the 'pope of Marxism' and who broadly shared this 'progressive' vision of history with liberal intellectuals (although the content of the progress sought was obviously different).

Such an ideology has become untenable, mainly because of the chaotic and murderous history of the twentieth century. Unless we consider this 'century of extremes' – to use the term used by the historian Eric Hobsbawm – as some sort of interval on the well-marked path of socialism, then the two World Wars, fascisms and their crimes (obviously first and foremost the genocide of the Jews of Europe), the bureaucratic degeneration of the USSR and its appalling consequences, or the massacres associated with the colonial wars, are all some of the many incomprehensible relapses into an archaic barbarity. But blind adherence to 'Progress' is also made unthinkable by the ecological crisis, of which climate change is the most evident symptom, and whose disastrous effects are still ahead of us. This crisis obviously imposes on us a necessary and urgent reflection on the consequences of what has long been perceived as the unquestioned source of human progress, including within a particular stream of Marxism, namely industrial development with its accompanying mass consumerism.[195]

But the crisis that we face is also social and political. It is a social crisis because of the consequences of the neoliberal policies pursued by governments since the 1980s until today and in the future for the majority of the population. These are aimed at reversing all the social gains of the workers' movement in the twentieth century that had made work and life a little less harsh for the working class (in particular with public services, social security and labour rights). It is also a political crisis because such destructive policies cannot fail to provoke opposition in very diverse forms (active or passive, emancipatory or reactionary). The current fascist danger can only be understood in the context of this political crisis, which in France has acquired the dimension of what Gramsci called a crisis of hegemony, that is of a growing inability of the ruling class to produce the consent of large sections of the population to its domination and its policies. The deliberate destruction by successive governments of the post-war social compromise has led not only to the deterioration of the living conditions of the working class, but also to the disintegration of all the mediations between the capitalist state – guarantor of the stability of bourgeois rule – and the population.

The most striking expression of this crisis is undoubtedly the way in which the French political field has been shaken up in a few years, and the same could be said, for example, of Italy. In France, we have seen the collapse of the two main parties that had dominated the

Fifth Republic and had governed French capitalism for nearly four decades: the Gaullist party (the RPR, which became the UMP and then *Les Republicains*), and the Socialist Party. We have also seen the strengthening of the electoral performance of neo-fascism (the *Front National*, which became *Rassemblement National*), the emergence of new political forces without a real militant network and stable electoral support (*La République En Marche* and *France Insoumise*), and the breakthrough of the ecologists in the 2019 European elections but without deep organizational roots in the population.

No one can predict how the political situation will develop in the years to come and I do not aspire here to formulate yet another prophesy that would only satisfy the taste for fear or the need for easy reassurance. Fascism, like insurrection, does not come in the form of an irresistible force. It is therefore less important to interpret the warning signs than to discover the conditions for its development, without giving into the temptation of a catastrophism that would disarms rather than mobilize, while still trying to grasp what is most chilling in our situation. How can we therefore not think of Trotsky predicting that the Second World War would inevitably mean the genocide of the Jews of Europe (unlike so many other intellectuals who advised against being alarmed or so many politicians who refused asylum to Jews fleeing Germany)? Given the particularly worrying and frenzied rise of Islamophobia in Western Europe (but also elsewhere, such as in India and China), and the parallels that can be drawn between Islamophobia today and antisemitism at the beginning of the twentieth century, there is plenty to justify being actively vigilant (and a response in the political field, which began with the march of 10 November last year).[196]

There is therefore no question of proposing a political fiction, but of highlighting what, in the current situation, is still embryonic, in fragments. Thus, the category of the possible, which was dear to

Daniel Bensaïd, must be emphasized to allow us to enrich our understanding of reality.[197] Focussing on the possible(s) enables us to uncover some hidden capacities for the transformation of societies, and makes room for the uncertain and unpredictable dynamic of the social and political balance of power. While this concept has been reassessed very positively in recent years[198], one should be careful not to restrict its use to the salutary irruption of emancipatory politics or to the construction of concrete alternatives (what Erik Olin Wright called 'real utopias'). The lateral possibilities mentioned previously are not only about human progress and the liberation of the oppressed. It is also important to consider and identify the possible morbid symptoms: the sudden onset of disaster or the gradual slide towards catastrophe. If the 'the chapter of bifurcations remains open to hope', as Blanqui wrote at the end of the Commune, so does it of chaos and despair.[199]

This brings us back to the Bensaïdian conception of history mentioned above, which supposes not counterposing the possibility of an event (beneficial or disastrous) to the inertia of economic and social structures. It is precisely when structures are put into crisis that the event becomes possible (for better or for worse). If history is a field of possibilities, some of which are clearly nightmares for millions of individuals and entire peoples, it is also a battlefield, which obliges us to act urgently, without guarantees or promises. History only offers a road map to the orphans of the great prophecies (religious or secular), who desperately seek a path marked out forever and the promise of a bright future. To others, it shows possible, occasional and limited trajectories – including disastrous ones. But that is already a lot! One of the major factors in these trajectories is of course the possibility of collective action by the millions of exploited and oppressed people who, on a national scale as well as that of humanity as a whole, make up the majority.

Ideas do not make the world go round, nor are they ever enough to change it, but in the process of the oppressed coming into action, a common understanding of these conditions (and an acute awareness of the dangers) can be a useful, if not an irreplaceable, instrument for developing an appropriate strategy. That is why, working from the concept of fascism is not a mere whim, but it can allow us to discover a continuity in an apparently chaotic history, build a common understanding and a shared memory, and renew the link between past, and present or future struggles. Without such an effort, fixing a potential anchor point and formulating strategic hypotheses seem impossible because they are without purpose. How do we know where we are and where to go if we delight in the illusion that we come from nowhere and we start from scratch at every moment? On the contrary, Daniel Bensaïd liked to remind us – quoting Deleuze – that 'we always start again from the middle', rejecting both the temptation of an immaculate beginning and the illusion of political models inherited from history, complete with instruction manuals.[200] Instead of a manual, better a compass.

19

The new wave of feminism

HEGOA GARAY AND ARYA MERONI

We must never fail to put into their context the comments to which we are trying to respond. This is especially the case when the time that separates us from these remarks has seen rapid, radical and unexpected developments. If internationally the feminist movement is today a driving force of the class struggle, ten years ago the situation was somewhat different. We seemed then to be at a low ebb, and this is noticeable in Daniel's interview. He rightly noted the disappearance of feminist publications and the retreat of campaigning organizations. These had suffered from almost twenty years of institutionalization of the women's movement and from the neoliberal hijacking of our victories. But instead of turning his thoughts to the major challenge which is the emancipation of half of humanity, Daniel remains in the interview in a certain 'comfort zone'. He chooses to pay homage to the exemplary militancy of class struggle feminists from our current in the 1970s and 1980s, and dwells on the stunning machismo of the post-war French Communist Party. Finally, when it comes to establishing the link between feminism and Marxism, he limits his remarks by focusing exclusively on Marx and Engels, forgetting to mention those who are references for many feminists today, such as Clara Zetkin or Alexandra Kollontai, to name but two. He even dares a dubious oxymoron by referring to Marx as an 'enlightened male chauvinist'. Yet it should not be a question of accusing or defending Marx, but rather of understanding how women, by virtue of their place in the complexity of domination and exploitation, have a central role to play in the struggle for emancipation. Daniel does understand the feminist movement as an integral part of the class struggle, which has enabled him to analyse its role as a driving force in history. It thus seemed to us necessary to extend his reflections and to bring to the forefront the revolutionary potentialities of the current feminist movement.

The world is going through a period of combined crises: destruction of life, climate change, increasing social inequalities, wars. We are witnessing a dramatic rise of extreme right-wing governments. Bolsonaro, Trump and Putin are the cornerstone of the global reactionary current that is waging war on the working classes, women, racialized people, LGBT, migrant women and the planet. In this global chaos, the international women's movement is being reborn in an extraordinary way. It is, as Daniel Bensaïd says, the product of a political fermentation. This movement took root in the countries of the South or the periphery (Argentina, Poland), then gradually reached the countries of the North hardest hit by the crisis (Spanish state, Italy) before finally reaching the richest countries (Switzerland, Belgium, France). In a way, the feminist movement follows the same path as commodities do in the era of globalized neo-liberalism. It can also be as if feminism had become a 'virus' which is seeking to go back to the centre of capitalism in order to destroy it.

DANIEL BENSAÏD

Combined oppositions: 'a combination, a bouquet, a sheaf finally of forms of resistance'[201]

We cannot consider feminism as a uniform whole that would fight against a single 'oppression'. Whenever we seek to identify and destroy oppressions, we need to understand them in their entirety. Oppressions do not follow one another, nor are they in opposition to each other.[202] There is not, as Daniel Bensaïd points out, a primary contradiction counterposed to secondary contradictions. Oppressions combine, merge, and constitute a whole that must be fought against in its entirety, without ever privileging one oppression over another. Even when the international struggle against violence against women is propelled to the front of the global political stage, this does not mean that other oppressions, and the struggles that accompany them, must disappear from our political agenda. This can be state racism and Islamophobia which continues to rage, extractivist policies that are destroying the Earth, LGBTIQ people who are being murdered daily or class violence that is still here. A consistent feminism must integrate all these issues and be at the same time anti-capitalist, anti-racist, internationalist, inclusive, decolonial and eco-socialist.

Reasoning in this way helps us in the struggle against a hegemonic and rigid pattern of thinking. A feminist theory and practice that is not always in motion would, objectively, come to exclude those it seeks to defend. Women themselves must do this theorizing. Indeed, who better placed than those concerned to decide how to put into words and concepts the violence they suffer and to decide on the type of resistance and struggle that corresponds to their needs.

Production and reproduction: a unified process for capital

Women's work in the capitalist world is often invisible. It is precarious, poorly paid or unpaid, and informal. In any case, it is almost completely absent from bourgeois economic analysis and is erased by politicians. In addition to the not insignificant part of the wage labour represented by women, all the reproductive work done in and outside the home seems to fall from the sky and to be part of the natural order of things. This is not the case. We often hear the word 'work' as the place, or even the time, where we have to be dedicated to the production of goods in return for a wage. But capitalism not only needs to produce commodities, it also needs to produce 'individuals'. Capitalism needs everyone to be fit to go to work every day, but it also literally needs to produce new workers ready for employment by corporations after a few years of 'intensive care'. Let us not forget that for capital, children are not the only source of potential workers, there is also total or partial slavery, as well as chosen or forced migration. The production of goods must therefore be understood as a process which is unified with that of reproduction. There is no separate sphere between production and reproduction. Capital controls the sphere of production and constantly controls the worker when she takes off her apron and goes home. This is an awful reality which nevertheless offers an infinite terrain of struggle for those who understand that the private is political, and that all the spaces of our lives are potentially spaces of rebellion and of class struggle.

DANIEL BENSAÏD

Feminism: a legitimate political leadership for the class

Of course, the movement is not free of contradictions and it is not a question of repainting it entirely in red. Natalie Portman and the Argentinian women mobilising for abortion rights[203] do not evolve in the same reality, and the media coverage of the feminism of one is often at the detriment of the actual conditions of the other. The revolutionary potential of feminism, as Daniel Bensaïd rightly pointed out, is not to be found in the search for a way for 'a smattering of privileged women to climb the corporate ladder'[204], nor has it been carried forward by laws for parity. Rather, we find it out of the spotlights: in neighbourhood assemblies in the Spanish state, in the meetings of *Ni Una Di Meno* in Italy, in the national co-ordinations in preparation for the 8 March general strike in Chile, or in the women-only assemblies in preparation for the general strike last December in Toulouse and Paris. The current frameworks of the autonomous women's movement are all potential spaces for the development of a feminism for the 99%: an anti-racist, anti-capitalist, eco-socialist, internationalist, inclusive and decolonial feminism.[205] If it is understood in this way, the autonomous women's movement is no longer just a women-only decision-making space for the feminist movement independent of unions, parties and the state; it is the self-organized political leadership of a movement that explicitly or implicitly demands a social revolution.

Eco-socialism and feminism: 'Defence of the body-Earth-territory'.

Women are among the main resisters to the neoliberal violence against individuals and nature, especially in the global South. They are those who cultivate the land in the Philippines or in Bangladesh, or who resist the mining companies in the Guatemalan mountains.[206] The latter define themselves as community feminists and weave a web between the body, the territory and the Earth. Their slogan is 'Defend the body-Earth-territory'. Women are therefore the first bulwark against the monopolization of bodies and territories, given their particular position in the system of production-reproduction. They are the ones who suffer most directly from the deterioration of the climate and from land evictions. They are the ones in the front line of the struggles. The body-territory refers to sexual violence and femicide which specifically affects women and children. The current wave of international mobilization around these issues only confirms the interest that we must take in the knowledge and the experience of these women. They establish a dialectical relationship between violence and the struggle to defend the environment: defending the Earth without caring about the violence that individuals on this same earth suffer would make no sense at all.

Lorena Cabnal sees the body as 'a political power for emancipation'.[207] Women's bodies are a playground for all oppressions and therefore must be considered as subjects of resistance. It is therefore these bodies, in struggle, that will confront the state, the military and the drug traffickers. At the same time, these bodies, that are subjected to violence, are the primary instrument of women's liberation. Women and women's bodies are therefore intimately linked to the Earth. They cultivate it, and are the first victims of private property and of environmental destruction. They stand up against the new wave of dispossession of the commons. They are the major political actors of the eco-socialist project, and we must take care to include them whenever possible in the process of reflection and of decision-making.

DANIEL BENSAÏD

Women: a political actor to overthrow capitalist hegemony

Daniel Bensaïd recalls the energy of the feminist press in the 1970s. Today, it has almost disappeared in France. In Latin America and in the Spanish state, we are seeing the blossoming of numerous feminist magazines and fanzines (most of them online or self-published) in which there is political reflection, literature, drawings and poetry. The development of the internet allows a rapid and wide distribution of the political agenda of our struggles but also of the progress of each other's reflections. This encourages more regular and varied exchanges of experiences and thoughts between feminists in the South and the North. We need to understand the strength of the internet and of the international feminist movement when a simple choreography[208] of feminist activists against the state and the rapes perpetrated by the Chilean *carabinieros* travels around the world, forming a wave of solidarity between women from different feminist movements.

Daniel Bensaïd speaks of 'deep-lying events that continue to work through'. By making the preparation of the 8 March strike a process that allows for a 'permanent state of feminist agitation', the activists of feminist self-organization around the world are waging a war of position against neoliberal hegemony, breaching the walls of cities, the shelves of libraries, the minds of new generations. The prevalence of feminism and the accumulation of actions or of frameworks for discussion at all levels help to create a climate conducive to feminist awareness by all women and the construction of a political cause.

Overcoming obstacles on the left: towards a 'permanent state of feminist agitation'.

As mentioned earlier, the self-organized feminist movement has re-emerged dramatically in different contexts but with common features. One of these is the existence of a specific mobilization against violence against women and femicide, or in defence of abortion rights. Another is the resistance and sometimes confrontation with sections of the traditional labour movement that are wary of the resurgence of a movement that it has never been able to control. For example, the trade unions in the Spanish State called for a 24-hour strike for 8 March 2019 only the day before, under pressure from hundreds of thousands of women workers who had announced that they would go on strike with or without their approval.

We are also interested in the role of *Nous Toutes* in France. Impelled by Caroline De Haas in the summer of 2018 in the wake of the Me Too movement, this collective is supported by the remnants of social democracy, trade unions and a large part of civil society. It benefits from political, media and economic support. The collective plays a contradictory role in the development of a mass feminist movement in France. *Nous Toutes* disseminates on a very large scale the true reality of violence against women, which in turn accelerates feminist awareness in the country. But it does not wish to develop a 'permanent state of feminist agitation' because it tends towards a mainstream feminism compatible with institutions whose achievement would be the election of a woman president. Thus, *Nous Toutes* does not push either for the construction of frameworks for self-organization or for the construction of general movements[209] that would allow feminism to be considered as a global struggle. On the contrary, revolutionary Marxist feminist activists must sincerely and fully commit themselves to the construction of an anti-capitalist, internationalist, decolonial, anti-racist and inclusive feminist movement, and thus contribute to the emergence of women as a political actor capable of being the accelerator of the class struggle.

Feminism in Chile: an accelerator of the class struggle

The example of the Chilean popular uprising in 2018 and the central role of the 8M Feminist Coordination (CF8M) within it is remarkable in this regard. The feminist mobilization against sexual violence initiated by female students in April 2018 has enabled thousands of Chilean women to become aware of their strength and their capacity for action 'in the struggle and through the struggle, during the revolution in progress', to use a formula from Rosa Luxemburg. In the year that followed, the self-organization of women in the CF8M and the preparation of the strike of 8 March maintained 'the permanent state of feminist agitation'. This was achieved by proposing frameworks for collective action, which are a far cry from neo-liberal individualism, in other words to constitute themselves as political actors capable of pulling the rest of the class along. This constituted 'something brewing, coming to the surface'[210] so that feminism could become a carrier for the reconstruction of class consciousness through the method of the strike. This was confirmed on 21 October 2019 when we witnessed a conjunction of the spontaneous uprising of the Chilean proletarian classes paralysing the country, and the accumulation of experiences and tools of mobilization pushed by the CF8M that forced the rest of the social and trade union movement to do the same.

It would be wrong to consider that the feminist movement has been won over to the need for an ecosocialist revolution. However, this new wave of feminism is emerging from the resistance of those who have decided to stand together against macho and neo-liberal violence and who choose to claim international sisterhood in the face of savage individualistic competition. It should be noted that these movements are fighting for the extension of individual and collective rights at a time when human rights have been eroded to the benefit of capital.[211] It should also be noted that, at the international level, the movement has chosen the feminist general strike as a strategy for struggle, challenging the traditional rules of understanding of the labour movement. However, it is a strike in the traditional sense of the term. It is impossible to think of a global uprising without including the labour power of women and children. The feminist strike is to be understood as a process of destruction of the relations of exploitation and oppression that affect all the spaces of our lives.[212] The problems highlighted by the strike lead to the questioning of patriarchy and capitalism as the origin and the driving force of alienation.

20

Daniel, end and continuity

OLIVIER BESANCENOT

It is difficult, if not impossible, to say goodbye to a dear friend like Daniel, especially since it will be unfortunately in the weeks, months and years to come that his political absence will be felt most acutely.

The void that he leaves in the field of political theory should be an urgent wake up call to seek to continue the work he had been doing for many years.

It is therefore impossible to close this beautiful gathering in the Mutualité, first and foremost because Daniel was not frankly the type to want to close anything, and anyway I think that he would not have appreciated that we leave except in a state of mind of wanting to continue his adventure, which is our adventure, a human and militant adventure.

I would like to keep as a memory of Daniel his tenacity, his steadfast commitment, his warmth, his incredible energy, his theoretical vigour and also the disconcerting ease with which he translated complex ideas into such accessible speeches.

Keeping this memory of Daniel, first of all it is a way to relieve our pain, and that is already not a bad thing, but above all it is a reminder that the fundamental reasons that motivated him throughout his life as a militant, are the same reasons that still make us want to act today. For him and for us, injustices are absolutely intolerable, and unlike so many others we have not given up on changing the world.

I think there is an expression that sums up what Daniel was: he was a carrier of fuel for thinking and action. For my generation, which was won over to militancy in the late 1980s, that means a lot, and it makes sense. There were a few of us who gained a political consciousness between two periods, two political centuries.

The previous century had been opened by the Russian revolution in 1917, and then there is the new century, which began with the fall of the Berlin Wall and the capitalist restoration in the countries of the East. Straddling these two periods, we were only a few hundred trying to clear a path that leads to a commitment to anti-capitalism. On this path, many of us came across Daniel.

First of all he helped us to clear the way, to understand, decipher, decode the mysterious workings of the capitalist system and its madness. But he did not just help us to clear the way, he also showed us, with his usual elegance, a road, a direction, or at least a track, that of action. Because indeed the goal is not just to understand the world, it is to change it. And Daniel's real strength is that he was able to do all this, at a time when it was so complicated.

At the beginning of the 1990s, we were working in times that were not easy, that were seeing tumultuous upheavals, a capitalism that was the great winner of history, and 'the impassable horizon of humanity'. The times grew darker with renunciations, disillusionment, disenchantment, retreats and withdrawals, and there was a ferocious economic aggressiveness of our adversaries, the new masters of the world. In short, in these rather dark times, Daniel came to enlighten our discussions with all his political culture and thinking. At a time when there was the great unanimous clamour of *la pensée unique*, he made his little voice, our little voice, ring out with a different sound. It was a breath of fresh air: his voice was soft, with a beautiful accent. He spoke with lyricism, but he did not concede anything, he did not give up any of the political fundamentals and, above all, he did not sing to the political tunes that were so fashionable. Marxism, that is what I am talking about, is what Daniel bequeathed to our generation. He knew how to share it with us, because Daniel was a sharer. He was even for sharing Marxism!

He was for sharing it with us, not as a sacred dogma, but as Marxism that should be and remain the very opposite of a fixed dogma, one that is in perpetual movement, continuously reassessed, and as close as possible to the contradictions of the reality of the world of today in which we live.

So all the theoretical work which he did was not only for him to keep jealously or for confrontations with a few initiated. He delivered his work publicly so that all those who wished, could pick it up and discover it. I believe that in this respect, I am not only speaking on my own behalf, but I am probably speaking for hundreds and perhaps thousands of people.

In those days, Daniel helped us to be militants while standing up to those, and I remember that there were many of them, who were there as grand prosecutors, obediently repeating great pleas from the important trials of history. In truth, they were using the trials of what had happened in the East to put all revolutionary ideas and all ideas of social transformation on trial. Daniel repeatedly said that these prosecutors were creating a deliberate confusion, and enjoyed putting on the same bench the revolutionaries and the counter-revolutionaries, the Stalinists and the anti-Stalinists, the executioners and the victims. In these painful moments, he made us want to continue and to believe, and that was no small thing.

It is now in a personal capacity that I would like to say, Daniel, thanks for your writings, your pamphlets and your small and large meetings. You helped me at that time to claim proudly, no longer half-heartedly, without being ashamed, of being a communist, a Marxist, and a revolutionary.

For that, I want to thank you, because this journey between the generations you did it, as you did many journeys in other fields. You also made journeys within the LCR and within the Fourth International, in your philosophical polemics, through your contributions to the social movement that was awakening in 1995, in your constant participation in the anti-globalization movement where you also tried to resurrect a discussion of strategic questions. I remember that you were one of the first I heard say: another world is possible, that's right, but we have to start saying which one. You carried on your journey until the rehabilitation of the Marxist analyses in which you participated during the financial and international crisis that we are still experiencing today.

Your journey took you into all sorts of fields, and you passed on your ideas, and our ideas, without flagging or getting tired, or in any case without giving up. You passed on our ideas without tiring others, something that is not common in militant circles and that makes all the difference. It is an open secret that Daniel liked and was even greedy for polemics. He was always waiting for that, but he did so with respect for the positions of others, and even better than that, he involved and pushed others to get involved in discussions. This is an absolutely irreplaceable quality in militancy and friendship.

There were friendships in his activism. With him, activism remained human and it is not by chance that Daniel was and remains a rallying point for people from such different horizons and backgrounds, and beyond borders, because he did not like borders. He did not like geographical borders, he did not like the borders between the manual world and the intellectual world, he did not like the borders between generations. That is why the age difference between us, for example, did not matter. He was able to build this bridge for people who successfully learned to live side by side through him.

This galaxy, because that is what we should call it, your galaxy, the Bensaïd galaxy, had a social and political reach that went far beyond the ranks of our party. I think the greatest tribute we could pay to him is to ensure that this galaxy survives, that this bridge is maintained, that these journeys continue.

However, there was one journey that Daniel could not stand, and that was that of the handover, the passing of the baton. Because when you hand over the baton, that means you have to stop, that means you have to let others do something you are no longer involved in. That was definitely not Daniel's style. Because he was living in his time, with his times: his activism was in the present. That is why he took an active part in all the stages of our organization, both internal and external, even during the most painful personal moments for him. That is why it is no coincidence that he was one of the most enthusiastic to launch the NPA, without any form of nostalgia. He sought, according to the expression he liked to use, to sublimate the LCR into it.

He did all that. I remember an anecdote when in 2002, he saw me in a new light as a presidential candidate. We had a long discussion, and I think he was as surprised as I was. He invited me with his sparkling eyes, as always, in his universe, that of ideas, of great historical lineages, of great contemporary polemics. Everything was being unravelled in front of me, Péguy, Sorel, Gramsci, Marx. It did not stop. It went on and on. And at one point, when he mentioned the thorny problem of rupture and continuity, just that, when he also talked about our relationship to the intellectual crisis, and when he noticed that I was beginning to flounder badly, he told me that there will at least be a continuity, the continuity of the relationship to ideas and the presidential candidate, because I have the impression that Alain [Krivine] and you have more or less the same profile. I do not know what profile he meant, but Daniel also had that *'joie de vivre'* that you have to keep.

Daniel was, you were, you are and you will remain, this permanent challenge against renunciation and resignation, because for you the fight had to go on, again and again.

Indeed, the fight continues today, again and again, and for this fight, his friendship, his pretty little laugh, his simplicity and his political thinking must help us to continue to believe in it.

So Daniel, I say to you one last time: *Hasta la victoria, Siempre!*

Transcript of Olivier Besancenot's speech at the tribute ceremony to Daniel Bensaïd, on 24 January 2010 at the Mutualité, Paris.

NOTES

1. The 18th National Congress of the French Section of the Workers' (Second) International, or SFIO, in December 1920. There was a split between the communist majority that joined the Third International and the minority that stayed as the SFIO.
2. Ernst Glaeser (1902-1963). Originally close to the German CP, his books were burned by the Nazis. He returned from exile in 1939 and supported the Nazis, hence the fact that his work is not well known.
3. *October: Ten Days that Shook the World*, a film made for the tenth anniversary of the revolution, banned in France from its first screening it became a myth: it was only in 1966 that its complete version became available to the general public.
4. 1981 film on the life of the communist activist John Reed, journalist and author of *Ten Days That Shook the World*.
5. Written in August-September 1917.
6. Furet is a Stalinist historian who moved to the SP, then to liberalism.
7. On the German revolution see the following interview.
8. Joseph de Maistre (1753-1821) a counter-revolutionary philosopher and thinker, much appreciated on the extreme right.

NOTES

9. Written in 1920.
10. The Third International or Comintern, founded in March 1919, brought together the communist parties supporting the Russian Revolution.
11. Livorno Congress of the Italian Socialist Party of January 1921, during which the minority in favour of joining the Third International split to found the Communist Party.
12. A formula taken from Gilles Deleuze (1925-1995), French philosopher.
13. The Freikorps was a paramilitary corps composed of several tens of thousands of well-armed and trained counter-revolutionary soldiers and officers, financed by the bosses, set up by the social democratic government which could not use the army to fight the revolutionary uprising. They crushed the German revolution and were at the origin of the first fascist paramilitary groups.
14. The Constituent Assembly elected in Russia on 12 November 1917, meeting in January 1918, was dissolved by the government of the soviets.
15. Edward Bernstein (1850-1932), theorist of revisionism, supporter of National Unity in 1914.
16. Karl Kautsky (1854-1938) considered within the Second International as the continuator of Marx's thought. Kautsky wrote in *The Road to Power*, published in 1909, 'The Socialist party is a revolutionary party, but not a revolution-making party. We know that our goal can be attained only through a revolution. We also know that it is just as little in our power to create this revolution as it is in the power of our opponents to prevent it. It is no part of our work to instigate a revolution or to prepare the way for it.'

17. During the Russian revolution of 1905, political and/or economic mass strikes, mostly spontaneous, played a decisive role, which led Rosa Luxemburg to write "Mass Strike, Parties and Trade Unions" in 1906. The Belgian general strike of April 1913 for universal suffrage was carefully organized by the Socialist Party.
18. Antonie Pannekoek (1873-1960) played an important role in the German and Dutch socialist movement, one of the theorists of council communism.
19. Written by Marx in 1875, it criticized the programme of the congress for the unification of the socialists in Germany. It was not published until after his death in 1891.
20. *The Crisis of Social Democracy*, written under the pseudonym Junius, describes the reasons for the failure of the Second International, defines revolutionary perspectives and introduces the fundamental idea of 'socialism or barbarism'.
21. Ségolène Royal (born 1953) is a French Socialist Party politician. Presidential candidate in 2007, she was beaten in the second round by Nicolas Sarkozy.
22. All socialist deputies voted for the war credits in the Reichstag on 4 August 1914, even those who were opposed to it. Liebknecht voted alone against the military budgets on 3 December 1914, there were two votes against in March 1915, and twenty on 29 December.
23. There were in fact 90 daily newspapers and hundreds of party publications. The SPD had 1 million members in 1914, the trade unions linked to the party had 4 million members; in addition there were hundreds of cultural, sports and other associations.

24. In 1921, at the instigation of the representative of the Third International, in order to 'force the development of the revolution', the German Communist Party called for a general strike and for armed action, without success.
25. Newspaper of the SPD whose leadership had ousted the editors critical of the war to lift its suspension by military authority in 1916. The Spartacists wanted 'their' newspaper back.
26. Closely linked to Rosa Luxemburg from Poland, Léo Jogiches was the main organizer of the Spartacus League.
27. Paul Lévy was one of the main leaders of the Communist Party. In prison at the time of the March 1921 action, he could not prevent it, but condemned it, publicly opposing the policy of the Third International from which he was excluded.
28. In this case, Bela Kun.
29. The October 1923 uprising was called off at the last moment. All the militants were warned, except those in Hamburg who rose up alone. Valtin's book is an exceptional testimony about the communist struggle in Germany in the 1920s and 1930s.
30. In Italy, revolutionary thrust of the red belt with workers' councils were elected in all the large factories in the industrial north, until the generalized occupation in August-September 1920. The Bavarian republic was proclaimed in April 1919, and crushed the following month by the *Freikorps*. The Hungarian republic was also established in April 1919, it was crushed in August 1919 by the nationalists. In Austria there were major social movements with elections for workers' councils and a socialist government (41% in the

1919 elections) which introduced very advanced social legislation.
31. Republican town in the Basque country destroyed in April 1937 by the German air force.
32. Novel published in 1947.
33. George Orwell (1903-1950). *Homage to Catalonia*, recounts the experience of the author, a fighter in the POUM.
34. *Land and Freedom*, a film by Ken Loach, released in 1995.
35. Members of the POUM (Workers' Party for Marxist Unification), born from the merger in 1935 of two non-Stalinist currents in Catalonia, dissolved after the revolutionary days of May 1937 in Barcelona and violently persecuted
36. Julián Grimau (1920-1963), one of the main Stalinist leaders of the PCE executed by the Francoist regime.
37. Republican victory against the Italian fascist army.
38. *Schutzbunden* (Republican Protection League) insurrection: armed confrontations between socialist workers and army-backed fascists.
39. Francisco Largo Caballero (1869-1946) member of the PSOE (Spanish Socialist Workers Party) and the UGT (General Union of Socialist Workers). Head of the Spanish government and minister of war from September 1936 to May 1937.
40. Andreu Nin Pérez (1892-1937) was one of the founders of the POUM and a close associate of Leon Trotsky.
41. José Buenaventura Durruti Dumange (1896-1936) was a Spanish anarchist, member of the CNT and fighter in Aragon.

NOTES

42. The Chinese Communist Party entered the *Kuomindang* led by Chiang Kai-shek in 1924. In February 1927 the Communists led a victorious insurrection in Shanghai, opening the doors to Chiang Kai-shek's army who massacred them. These massacres happened again in May in Wuhan and in December in Canton: it is estimated that 38000 communists were liquidated in cold blood in 1927. The Red armies regrouped to survive in the south with Mao Zedong.
43. Victor Serge born Victor Lvovich Kibalchich (1890-1947). Anarchist, he supported the Russian revolution and joined the Russian Communist Party, then the Left Opposition.
44. Lev Sedov was Trotsky's son. Doubts remain about the circumstances of his death in 1938, an assassination by the NKVD or complications following a medical operation? Zinaida Volkova committed suicide in Berlin on 5 January 1933.
45. Documentary film released in 1963, partly censored by the French government at the request of the Spanish government.
46. The Battle of Stalingrad (July 1942 – February 1943) was a major defeat for the German army, the turning point in the Second World Wars. The Yalta conference in February 1945 (USA, Britain and USSR) ratified a plan to divide Europe into 'zones of influence', six months after the Potsdam conference organized the division of Germany into four zones.
47. Vasily Grossman (1905-1964). Communist author, his book was seized by the Stalinist political police in 1962.
48. This refers to Trotsky's founding of the Fourth International in 1938, based on very small groups. Previous con-

ferences were held in September 1915 (Zimmerwald) and April 1916 (Kienthal) among socialists opposed to national unity for the war. Despite their disagreements, this was the beginning of an alternative to the failure of the Second International.

49. 1957 Soviet film, *Palme d'or* at Cannes in 1958, a love story set in the Second World War which symbolizes the thaw in the USSR after Stalin's death in 1953.
50. 1985 French film on Communist activism in the 1950s.
51. While the influence rates determined at Yalta were 50-50%, the Yugoslav CP proclaimed a popular republic and resisted Soviet hegemony, which provoked a rupture in 1948. A new socialist road emerged around proclaimed self-management. Trials were launched against potential communist oppositionists to avert the Yugoslav contagion. These purges disappeared activists for their role in the International Brigades in Spain, such as Rajik in Hungary or Artur London in Czechoslovakia.
52. Dominique Eudes *Les Kapétanios: La Guerre civile grecque1943-49* Paris: Fayard 1970. Stratís Tsírkas *Drifting Cities* (trilogy *The Club, Ariagni, The Bat*) 1974.
53. In February 1945, under Soviet pressure (at Yalta, Greece was 'awarded' 90% to Britain) the Communists accepted the dissolution of the Resistance armed forces. The Franco-Chinese (or Chongqing) accord signed at Chongqing, on 28 February 1946, between the provisional government of the French Republic and the Republic of China. The accord foresaw the departure of Chinese troops stationed in Indochina, and the end of French concessions in China

(Shanghai, Hankou et Tsientsin) dating from unequal treaties

54. See note 41.
55. Independent Labour Party, formed by British pacifists breaking with the Labour Party, with links to the POUM. For Orwell see note 32.
56. Cornelius Castoriadis (1922-1997) was a Greek philosopher, economist and psychoanalyst who left the CP for the Fourth International, before leaving it in 1949 to found "Socialism or Barbarism', a group close to council communism which analysed the USSR as a form of state capitalism. Jean-François Lyotard (1924-1998) was a philosopher, anti-authoritarian communist, who took part in the beginnings of Socialism or Barbarism.
57. David Rousset was a Trotskyist activist deported to Buchenwald (1912-1997). He distanced himself from Trotskyism in the 1950s while continuing to actively oppose the Algerian war.
58. After the war for independence from 1945 to 1949 in Indonesia, nationalist currents that took a conservative, pro-Western line opposed those who wanted to bring in an economic, social and political democracy. In Vietnam against the resistance to the Japanese occupation, the United States installed a neocolonial structure.
59. Pandelis Pouliopoulos (1900-1943), general secretary of the Greek CP in 1924, leader of a Leninist opposition within the party and expelled. He was then editor of *Spartakos* and founding member of the Fourth International in Greece.
60. Tan Malaka (1897-1949) was an Indonesian nationalist and communist activist, executed by the army in 1949.

61. United Nations Economic Commission for Latin America and the Caribbean founded in 1948, with the aim of promoting industrialization of countries in the zone via regional integration instead of imports.
62. *La société éclatée. De la première à la première à la seconde révolution mondiale*, Paris: Éditions Grasset, 1973.
63. Published in 1962-1964. Louis Aragon (1897-1982) was the official-line Communist intellectual, André Maurois (1885-1967) president of the France–United States association. Five volumes; two for each country from 1917 to 1960, and the final volume made up of 'conversations'.
64. The first Congress of the Peoples of the East, with delegates from all the Eastern countries in September 1920.
65. Rif war: anti-colonial war in Morocco (1920s).
66. *Front de Libération National*, National Liberation Front, formed in 1954, leading force in the fight for independence.
67. 'Declaration on the right of insubordination in the Algerian War', September 1960.
68. *Mouvement National Algérien*, founded in 1954.
69. A French Algerian political-military organization, *Organisation armée secrète*, opposing Algerian independence.
70. Soummam was a clandestine FLN Congress held in August 1956. The three Bs: Lakhdar Bentobal, Abdelhafid Boussouf and Belkacem Krim.
71. Ahmed Ben Bella (first president of the republic) was overthrown by a coup led by Houari Boumédiène.
72. Guevara stated that mechanically copying the 'brother countries' was a mistake and slowed down development and led to bureaucratism which should be fought against

vigorously. See https://www.youtube.com/watch?v=kWNTvvoAja0
73. The 26 July Movement led the victorious insurgency.
74. Armand Gatti (1924-2017), French film-maker. This allegorical film of great creativity was made in 1963.
75. Climactic crisis of the Cold War that led to the brink of nuclear war after the installation in Cuba of Soviet missiles aimed at the United States. The crisis resulted in a direct USSR/USA negotiation without the Cubans, with the withdrawal of missiles from Cuba on one side and from Turkey and Italy on the other.
76. The Tricontinental, born in 1966, brought together anti-imperialist movements. A message from Che Guevara in 1967 called for the creation of two, three, many Vietnams, a break with the peaceful coexistence promoted by the USSR.
77. In 1966, Mao Zedong, who had been ousted following the catastrophe of forced collectivization and industrialization (there were at least 30 million deaths between 1958 and 1962), launched the 'Great Proletarian Cultural Revolution' to take over the leadership of the party. He mobilized the youth in the 'Red Guards' to purify the party, which attacked all hierarchies and traditional values. It lasted 10 years until the death of Mao Zedong in 1976.
78. 'To build communism it is necessary, simultaneous with the new material foundations, to build the new man and woman.'
79. Bolivarism is a Latin American anti-imperialist nationalist current, named after the revolutionary Simon Bolivar

(1783- 1830). José Marti (1853-1895) is a national hero in Cuba, martyr of independence.
80. Alejo Carpentier, *El Siglo de las Luces* (The Age of Enlightenment) 1962. Published in English under the title *Explosion in a Cathedral* 1963.
81. Amilcar Cabral (1924-1973) was founder of the *Partido Africano da Independência da Guiné e Cabo Verde* (PAIGC – African Party for the Independence of Guinea and Cape Verde). He was assassinated six months before the independence of Guinea Bissau.
82. Camilo Torres Restrepo (1929-1966) 'guerrilla priest', priest, sociologist and revolutionary, eventually joined the guerrilla, he was killed during his first military operation.
83. Ernesto Cardenal (1925-2020) A former monk and priest, he founded a utopian monastic community in 1965, then fought with the Sandinistas against the dictator Somoza.
84. Arnaldo T. Ochoa Sánchez (1930-1989) accused without evidence of embezzlement, corruption and drug trafficking, convicted after a self-criticism session.
85. Nicolae Ceaușescu (1918-1989), head of state in Romania from 1967 to 1989.
86. Sugar harvest, which mobilized the whole country for 18 months and failed to reach 8.5 million.
87. Tupamaros – movement that organized the armed struggle in Uruguay in the 1960s and 1970s.
88. Amilcar Cabral, see note 80.
89. At this conference, held between November 1884 and February 1885, the main European countries shared out Africa amongst themselves.

90. Jacques Roumain (1907-1944), poet, writer, and founder of the Haitian Communist Party. Aimé Césaire (1913-2008), long time the member of parliament of Martinique and mayor of Fort-de-France. He was an eminent poet who left a considerable body of work, with texts such as *Cahier d'un retour au pays natal* (1932) or *Moi, laminaire* (1982).
91. Frantz Fanon (1925-1961), psychiatrist born in Martinique, one of the theoreticians of Third-Worldism.
92. W.E.B. Du Bois (1868-1963), sociologist and historian, and one of the founders of the National Association for the Advancement of Colored People (NAACP) in 1909. C.L.R. James (1901-1989), intellectual from Trinidad and Tobago who joined the Left Opposition in Britain in the early 1930s.
93. Jean-Claude Milner (b. 1941), linguist and Maoist in his youth. Benny Levy (1945–2003), philosopher and former Maoist leader.
94. Mehdi Ben Barka (1920-disappeared 29 October 1965), socialist opponent of the king of Morocco, anti-imperialist and pan-African activist. He was kidnapped in Paris in 1965, his body was never found.
95. Georges Séguy (1927-2016) *Le Mai de la CGT* (1972).
96. Henri Weber (1944-2020) was one of the founders of the JCR, then of the Communist League (forerunner of the LCR) with Daniel Bensaïd and Alain Krivine, and one of the leaders of May 68. He left the LCR at the end of the 1970s and joined the PS in 1986.
97. Provos – anti-authoritarian network born in Amsterdam, a form of counter-culture, of global protest. Berkeley is a

prestigious university in California in which student mobilization played an important role in the civic movement against racial segregation in the USA in the 1960s, then in the struggle against US intervention in Vietnam. SDS – German Socialist Students' Union, which from the 1960s onwards became an anti-authoritarian organization, rejecting GDR socialism, its most famous leader was Rudi Dutschke.

98. The *Partido dos Trabalhadores* (PT) was founded in 1980 out of the desire of social, trade union and popular movements to have an independent socialist party, born out of resistance to the military dictatorship. In its early years, it was a radical mass organization that brought together the most active militants of all these movements.

99. The Prague Spring was the introduction of freedom of the press, of the right to assembly, of movement, of decentralization of the economy by the new communist leadership (Dubcek). This 'socialism with a human face' was crushed by an intervention of the Soviet army. The Tet Offensive of the Vietnam Liberation Front against the American and South Vietnamese armies took place in about a hundred cities. In spite of the military defeat, it was a strategic victory, a turning point in the war: the credibility of the United States collapsed and the position of the opposition to the American intervention in Vietnam was strengthened.

100. At the Olympics in Mexico City the African-American runners Smith and Carlos, supporters of the Black Panthers, first and third in the final of the 200 metres, protested at the medal ceremony against racial segregation in the United States by lowering their heads and raising clenched

fists. Three Cultures Square: student demonstration suppressed by the army.
101. Rudi Dutchske (1940-1979), following a violent press campaign he was the victim of an attack on 11 April 1968. He was very seriously wounded and died in 1979 from the sequels of this assassination attempt.
102. Daniel Cohn-Bendit a Franco-German activist who was a libertarian at the time. He moved away from a revolutionary perspective at the end of the 1970s and joined the German Greens in 1984. Today he supports Macron.
103. Tariq Ali, an anti-imperialist militant of Pakistani origin, in 1968 a member of the Fourth International group in Britain. Left in 1981 to support the left of the Labour Party.
104. Despite the signing of the Grenelle agreements on 27 May, the strikes continued, the Charléty meeting was held and the CGT organised a demonstration for a 'popular government' that brought out 500,000 people. The public rally of fifty thousand people on 27 May at the Charléty stadium was called by the UNEF, the CFDT, the FEN, on the initiative of the PSU. At the same time, Mitterrand announced he would stand for president and proposed Mendès France (who voted against the investiture of De Gaulle in 1958) as prime minister. The following day he declared himself willing to lead a government of the united left.

On 29 May, De Gaulle disappeared and went to consult General Massu in Baden Baden. It is now known that the latter advised De Gaulle to take the political offensive, convinced that the PCF did not want power under these conditions. On his return he announced the dissolution of the

National Assembly and organised the Gaullist demonstration of 30 May that rallied hundreds of thousands of people in support of the government and the President.
105. In Italy, the student and workers' mobilizations that began in 1968 continued for a decade, taking on very varied forms, with very important links between them.
106. The Renault factory had just been nationalized. Some thirty thousand people worked there, more than fifteen thousand of whom were members of the CGT. The strike was launched by Trotskyist militants against the advice of the CGT and the PCF, which was still in government (it was pushed out a month later), and was followed by a series of radical strikes throughout France.

    Pivertism was a revolutionary current emerging in the Socialist Party of the 1930s, then from 1938 onwards with the Socialist Workers and Peasants Party (PSOP).
107. Jacques Duclos (1896-1975) central leader of PCF. Gaston Defferre 1910-1986, SP mayor of Marseille for 33 years. Pierre Mendès France (1907-1982) at the time member of the PSU.
108. Successive secretaries of the CFDT in the 1990s/2000s after its 'refocusing' (*recentrage*), its transition to a trade unionism of negotiation against a trade unionism of struggle, excluding the class struggle currents.
109. Leader of the Hacuitex Federation, very combative social Christian, member of the PSU.
110. Chris Marker, film director and photographer who worked in popular culture associations, then in militant cinema from the 1960s onwards. The 1967 film chronicled strikes at the textile factory.

111. A review edited from 1961 to 1972 by François Maspero. *Libération des Femmes, Année Zéro* number 54-55, July-October 1970 and issue number 57 of January-February 1971, virtually all the articles dealt with this question.
112. Jeannette Vermeersch (1910-2001), Stalinist Communist leader distinguished in the 1950s by her stance against birth control and abortion and for a 'proletarian moral order'.
113. Flora Tristan (1803-1844), a socialist and feminist militant, a major figure of the time. Louise Michel (1830-1905), an anarchist and feminist militant, who played a significant role in the Paris Commune of 1871 and again after her return from New Caledonia.
114. Published in 1936, an analysis of the Soviet economy and society, in which he shows that it was neither a socialist nor a capitalist society.
115. In the order they are mentioned: A Quebecois publishing house created in 1975; the bulletin of the Flora Tristan circle created in 1973 became in 1975 *La cause des femmes*; journal published by the *Mouvement de Libération des Femmes* from 1971 to 1973; 'class struggle' feminist revolutionary Marxist review created in 1977 by the LCR.
116. The 1975 law proposed by Simon Veil legalized abortion under certain conditions for the first time. This followed a 1971 manifesto by 343 women stating that they had had an abortion, which was illegal, demanding the legalization of abortion and the trial in 1972 of a young woman who had an abortion after being raped, with a major effect since she was not sentenced: the law banning abortion could no longer apply,

117. The *Mouvement pour la Libération de l'Avortement et de la Contraception* was formed in 1973 with activists from the Family Planning, the women's liberation movement and the Health Information Group, it was disbanded in 1975 after abortion was legalized. On 6 October 1979, 50 thousand demonstrated for abortion rights.
118. The 'Psychanalyse et politique' current which postulated a natural difference between the masculine and the feminine. Fouque was a psychoanalyst and historic activist in the MLF.
119. Antonio Gramsci (1891-1937) founder of the Italian Communist Party, a major Marxist intellectual of the twentieth century, who elaborated a theory of cultural hegemony: the bourgeoisie dominates by force, but also by consent.
120. Published in 1884 based on Marx's notes.
121. Engels came from a textile factory-owning family in Manchester.
122. Salvador Allende (1908-1973), elected in 1970, head of Popular Unity, an electoral coalition of left-wing parties, died on 11 September 1973.
123. General Augusto Pinochet (1908-2006) led the Chilean coup d'état on 11 September 1973, establishing a dictatorship that lasted until 1988. In 1969, the Bolivian president nationalized the American company Gulf Oil, the mines, and agreed to hold a popular assembly with the workers' unions. This experience was crushed in blood by General Banzer's coup d'état on 21 August 1971.
124. The Sandinista National Liberation Front, founded in 1961, a political-military organization bringing together

Marxists and left-wing nationalists, overthrew the dictator Somoza in 1979.
125. The Indonesian Communist Party claimed 3 million members and 20 million in the organizations it controlled (workers, youth, peasants ...), it sought to take power legally, the repression was terrible: more than 700,000 dead, the party was physically destroyed. The Sudanese Communist Party was a major political force in the country. Following an abortive coup d'état, the communists were executed *en masse*, and the party was crushed.
126. MAPU (Unitary Popular Action Movement) an extreme left-wing Christian current which was a member of Popular Unity. MIR (Movement of the Revolutionary Left) revolutionary organization founded in 1965 by trade unionists and students, which, while preparing for armed action, supported Allende's government.
127. Luis Vitale (1927-2010). Argentinian who spent most of his life in Chile. Founder of the MIR but previously and subsequently a Fourth Internationalist.
128. This strike was supported financially by the US Secret Service and various multinationals.
129. Empty pots marches.
130. Carmen Castillo (born 1945 Santiago de Chile) is a writer and film-maker, in exile since the assassination of her husband, MIR general secretary, in 1974. Her film on Chile: *Calle Santa Fe* 2007. In 2015 she made a film on political activism *On est vivants*, inspired by the thinking of her close friend Daniel Bensaïd.
131. Argentinian military dictatorship 1976-1983.

132. Latin American Solidarity Organization, meeting in Havana in 1967.
133. The Somoza dynasty had controlled Nicaragua since 1937.
134. In 1967 and again in 1970, the FSLN suffered several military defeats, entering a 'silent phase of military build-up'.
135. Tomás Borge (1930-2012) resistance fighter to the Somoza dictatorship, refugee for a time in Cuba. Jaime Wheelock (b. 1946) leader of the Proletarian Tendency of the FSLN. Daniel Ortega (b. 1945) is the current president of Nicaragua.
136. By the Farabundo Marti National Liberation Front, in January 1981, November 1989, and July 1991.
137. Mario Payeras (1940–1995) *Days of the Jungle: The Testimony of a Guatemalan-Guerrillero, 1972-1976*.
138. Violetta Chamorro (b. 1929) leader of the opposition to the Sandinistas.
139. An Amerindian group present in an area where armed groups hostile to Sandinistas from Honduras were passing through, towards which the Sandinistas policy was violent, and a city in the area that is not accessible by road.
140. The strike called by the fifteen thousand-strong union was for a wage increase and a 32 hour working week of four days.
141. The strike lasted one year, from March 1984 to March 1985, against mine closures involving the loss of tens of thousands of jobs.
142. Jack Lang (b. 1939) a Socialist Party politician, minister of culture twice in the ten years following 1981.
143. The left got more than 50% in the first round: the Socialist Party and the Radicals were first with 24.9%, the Commu-

nist Party had 20.6%, the extreme left more than 3% and the ecologists more than 2%. However, the right won with more than 51% in the second round.

144. In April 1974 the Carnation Revolution brought down the dictatorship in power in Portugal since 1932, then the masses started a revolutionary process, the bourgeoisie, supported by the SP, took the situation in hand by taking decisive action in November 1975. In Spain there was the negotiated transition from the dictatorship after Franco's death in 1975, which installed a parliamentary democracy while maintaining the monarchy. In Italy the historic compromise between the two dominant parties, Christian Democracy and the Communist Party (more than 34% in the 1976 elections), aimed at a national government. It failed under pressure from the Vatican and the USA.

145. Notably the hiring of 55,000 civil servants, raising of the minimum wage and the minimum old-age pension, retirement at 60, fifth week of paid holidays, repayment of abortion fees, in addition to the abolition of the death penalty.

146. In Cancun in October 1981 Mitterrand advocated non-interference, the free self-determination of peoples, the peaceful resolution of conflicts and a new international order. De Gaulle in 1966 reaffirmed the 'right of peoples to self-determination' while the USA was fighting in Vietnam, in 1967 he proclaimed 'long live a free Quebec!'.

147. In October 1982, the Government taxed foreign (mainly Japanese) video recorders and subjected them to legal restrictions, a measure which was lifted after a year.

148. Lionel Jospin of the SP, beaten by Jacques Chirac for the right in the 1995 presidential elections, became Prime Min-

ister of a plural majority government including the Communists, after the electoral victory of the left in the 1997 legislative elections.
149. Benoît Frachon (1893-1975) leader of the PCF during the Occupation, had participated in the negotiation of the Matignon agreements in 1936 as a leader of the CGT. Secretary General of the CGT from 1945 to 1967.
150. Eric Hobsbawm, British Marxist historian. His trilogy of books on the twentieth century is essential reading.
151. *Rosa Luxemburg*, film by Margarethe Von Trotta, 1986.
152. For Karl Kautsky and Eduard Bernstein, see notes 15 and 16. August Bebel became President of the German Social Democratic Party in 1900. He was in the centre of the party between revolutionaries like Rosa Luxemburg and reformists like Bernstein.
153. Stéphane Courtois, former Maoist militant turned anti-communist, author of many books with contentious statistics on the crimes of communism.
154. Leonid Brezhnev (1906-1982) led the USSR from 1966 until his death in 1982. Yuri Andropov (1914-1984) was head of the political police, the KGB, under Brezhnev before succeeding him after his death.
155. Moshe Lewin (1921-2010), a historian specialising in the USSR where he lived until 1945. He was educated in the Soviet Union and had been a soldier in the Red Army.
156. Vladimir Zazubrin (1895-1937) wrote *Le Tchékiste* in 1923. It was banned despite the support of Gorky and finally published in French in 1990. It was made into a film *The Chekist* in 1992.

157. The New Economic Policy (NEP) was introduced at the end of the Civil War. It was a 'strategic retreat' that restored some private property, especially in agriculture, to restart the economy because Russia alone could not move to socialism.
158. *The Killing Fields*, by Roland Joffe (1984), is a film about the seizure of the country by the 'Khmer Rouge' with Pol Pot at their head. His dictatorial reign over Cambodia cost the lives of twenty per cent of the population.
159. Ernest Mandel (1923-1995) was a Belgian Marxist theorist and economist. He was one of the most important Trotskyist leaders of the second half of the twentieth century.
160. Nikolai Bukharin (1888-1938) was an early Bolshevik, a Marxist economist. He defended the NEP set up in 1921, then theorized the idea of 'socialism in one country'. A victim of the Stalinist trials of the 1930s, he was executed.
161. On 17 January 1991, a coalition of 35 states led by the United States invaded Iraq to challenge Iraq's invasion of Kuwait, even though having been warned of the invasion the US had declared that it would not intervene.
162. Erich Honecker (1912-1994) was the Stalinist leader of East Germany.
163. Karl Marx, Friedrich Engels *The German Ideology*, Part I: Feuerbach. Opposition of the Materialist and Idealist Outlook D. Proletarians and Communism – Individuals, Class, and Community.
164. Daniel Bensaïd, Olivier Besancenot, *Prenons parti. Pour un socialisme du XXIe siècle*, Paris: Mille et une nuits, p. 91.
165. The Walter Lippmann Colloquium was a conference of intellectuals organized in Paris in August 1938. The Mont

Pelerin Society (MPS) is an international neoliberal organization composed of economists, philosophers, historians, intellectuals and business leaders.

166. Ugo Palheta, Julien Salingue, 'Pour un recommencement communiste' in Bensaïd, Palheta, Salingue, *Stratégie et Parti*, Paris: Les Prairies ordinaires, 2016, p. 222.
167. 'Après 25 ans de néolibéralisme, comment remonter le courant ?' (After 25 years of neoliberalism, how can we get back on track?) *SolidaritéS*, No. 96, 1 November 2006.
168. *Prenons parti*, op. cit. p. 103.
169. 'Apres 25 ans de neoliberalisme, comment remonter le courant?', art. cit.
170. Gregoire Chamayou, *La Société ingouvernable. Une généalogie du libéralisme autoritaire*, Paris: La Fabrique, 2018, p. 267.
171. Daniel Bensaïd, *Les dépossédés. Karl Marx, les voleurs de bois et le droit des pauvres*, Paris: La Fabrique, 2007, p. 83.
172. Bensaïd, *Strategie and Parti*, op. cit. p. 129.
173. Sophie Bensaïd, 'Daniel Bensaïd intime', *Cahiers critiques de philosophie*, Hermann Éditeur, 2016, p. 176
174. Daniel Bensaïd, *Éloge de la politique profane*, Paris: Albin Michel, 2008, p. 9.
175. *Op cit* p.9
176. David Harvey, *A Brief History of Neoliberalism*, Oxford: Oxford University Press, 2007, p.21.
177. 'Trying to ward off the permanent threat of a decline in profitability by a dizzying headlong rush, capital seems determined to take over the monopoly of speed (circulation and accumulation): credit, advertising, marketing, and short-sighted speculation compete on a frenzied rhythm

with the accelerated repetition of its cycles. This frantic circulation of capital seems to force its critics into a deadly race of speed. [...] Rather than taking up this challenge and rushing headlong into the race to disaster, it becomes urgent to explore the steep paths of a revolution of deceleration and slowness and to imagine another cycle.' *Éloge de la politique profane*, p. 35.

178. 'Apres 25 ans de neoliberalisme, comment remonter le courant?', *art. cit.*
179. *Prenons parti*, op. cit., p. 261.
180. I. Garo, *Communisme et Strategie*, Paris: Editions Amsterdam, 2019, p. 275
181. *Prenons parti*, op. cit., p. 34
182. Amorim, L. Galastri, 'Théorie de la valeur, travail et classes sociales. Entretiens avec Daniel Bensaïd', May 2009.
183. Daniel Bensaïd, *Penser Agir*, Paris: Lignes, 2008, p. 305
184. Daniel Bensaïd, *An Impatient Life – A Memoir*, London: Verso, 2015, p.325.
185. 'Après 25 ans de néolibéralisme, comment remonter le courant ?' *art. cit.*
186. *Éloge de la politique profane*, op. cit. p. 8.
187. Daniel Bensaïd, *La politique comme art stratégique*, Paris: Syllepse, 2011, p. 114,
188. *Prenons parti*, op. cit, p. 240.
189. *Idem*, p. 266
190. Will Steffen, Paul J. Crutzen, John R. McNeil 'The Anthropocene: Are Humans Now Overwhelming the Great Forces of Nature', 2007.
191. 'Leaps – Leaps – Leaps', first published in *International Socialism* No 95, July 2002.

192. Ugo Palheta, *La Possibilité du fascisme. France : trajectoire du désastre*, Paris: La Découverte, 2018.
193. Published in English as *Marx for Our Times – Adventures and Misadventures of a Critique*, London: Verso 2010.
194. Daniel Bensaïd, *Walter Benjamin, sentinelle messianique*, Paris: Les Prairies Ordinaires, 2010 [1990].
195. See in particular the works (particularly in French) of Daniel Tanuro, Michael Löwy or Razmig Keucheyan, but also those in English of ecological Marxism by Andreas Malm, Jason Moore, and John Bellamy Foster.
196. On 10 November 2019, a March against Islamophobia took place in Paris with, depending on the source, between thirteen and forty thousand people, making this event an undeniable success.
197. Bachelard writes in *La valeur inductive de la réalité* that 'it is through the possible that we discover the real'.
198. For a discussion of this, see in particular: L. Jeanpierre, F. Nicodème and P. Saint-Germier, 'Possibilités réelles', *Tracés*, 2013, No. 24.
199. This is often quoted by Daniel Bensaïd, from 'Eternity Through the Stars', Auguste Blanqui.
200. On this point see *Stratégie et parti*, op cit.
201. Daniel Bensaïd in the episode 26 August 1970 of this book.
202. See on this subject Lise Vogel, *Marxism and the Oppression of Women: Toward a Unitary Theory*, Haymarket Books 2014, or the work of Cinzia Arruzza.
203. The struggle for abortion rights is a struggle of our class. In Argentina, for example, while the right to abortion is very restrictive, it is even more so for those who cannot afford to go abroad.

NOTES

204. Cinzia Arruzza, Tithi Bhattacharya, Nancy Fraser, *Feminism for the 99%, a manifesto*, London: Verso Books, 2019, p.11.
205. For example, the two manifestos for the 8 March strike of 2018 and 2019 included all these themes. Although opposed by liberal feminists and part of social democracy, this orientation mobilized millions of women on to the streets.
206. 80% of food crops in the global South are produced by women.
207. Guatemalan community feminist.
208. *Un violador en tu camino* by the Las Tesis collective
209. For example, the fight against pension reform, precariousness and labour law reforms, for solidarity with migrant women, or demonstrating against Islamophobia.
210. Daniel Bensaïd, episode 26 August 1970.
211. We are thinking in particular of the struggle for the right to abortion, for equal rights, for a law against violence against women, for the defence of public services, for the right and defence of the Earth.
212. Work, consumption, sexuality, care, territory, education, domestic work.

ABOUT RESISTANCE BOOKS AND THE IIRE

Resistance Books

Resistance Books is the publishing arm of Socialist Resistance. We publish books independently, and also jointly with Merlin Press (London) and the International Institute for Research and Education (Amsterdam). Further information about Resistance Books, including a full list of titles available and how to order them, can be obtained at www.resistancebooks.org.

Contact Resistance Books:
info@resistancebooks.org; www.resistancebooks.org
Resistance Books, PO Box 62732, London, SW2 9GQ.

Socialist Resistance is a revolutionary Marxist, internationalist, ecosocialist and feminist political network. Analysis and news from Socialist Resistance can be read online at www.socialistresistance.org. Socialist Resistance collaborates with the Fourth International, whose online magazine, *International Viewpoint*, can be viewed at www.internationalviewpoint.org.

The International Institute for Research and Education

The International Institute for Research and Education is a centre for the development of critical thought and the exchange of experiences and ideas between people engaged in their struggles. Since 1982, when the Institute opened in Amsterdam, its main activity has been the organisation of courses for progressive forces around the world. The seminars, courses and study groups deal with all subjects related to the emancipation of the oppressed and exploited around the world. It has welcomed participants from across the world, most of them from developing countries. The IIRE provides activists and academics opportunities for research and education in three locations: Amsterdam, Islamabad and Manila.

The IIRE publishes *Notebooks for Study and Research,* which focus on contemporary political debates, as well as themes of historical and theoretical importance. The *Notebooks* have appeared in several languages besides English and French. All the *Notebooks* are available by going to http://iire.org/en/resources/notebooks-for-study-and-research.html. Other publications and audio files of the events held at the IIRE are available in several languages and can be freely downloaded from www.iire.org.

Contact the International Institute for Research and Education:
iire@iire.org; www.iire.org; Phone: 00 31 20 671 7263
IIRE, Lombokstraat 40, Amsterdam, 1094 AL, The Netherlands.

www.ingramcontent.com/pod-product-compliance
Ingram Content Group UK Ltd.
Pitfield, Milton Keynes, MK11 3LW, UK
UKHW042003230426
12048UKWH00009B/524